MILAREPA

The Tibetan Poet-Mystic
& His Songs

MILAREPA

The Tibetan Poet-Mystic
& His Songs

Sunita Pant Bansal

Heritage Classics

HERITAGE PUBLISHERS
19-A, Ansari Road, Daryaganj, New Delhi - 110002
Tel: 23266258, 23264444
Fax: 23263050, E-mail: heritage@nda.vsnl.net.in

ISBN: 978-81-7026-262-6

Design & layout
SPB Enterprises Pvt. Ltd.
www.spbenterprises.net.in

Printed in India

Milarepa
(1051-1135)

Milarepa's story was written in the twelfth century by his disciple Rechungpa in Tibet. There are several versions of it. All end with the scene of old Milarepa about to die, who summons his disciples and addresses them with these words:

"Trust and pay attention to the law of karma that regulates causes and effects. Remember the impossibility to foresee our death and the punishments of the worldly life. Those who are full of worldly desires cannot do anything for other people's sake and cannot be helpful even to themselves.

Since space is unlimited and creatures are innumerable, you will always have the chance to act to advantage of others, when you are in a position to do it. Start by occupying the last place, give up clothes, food and words. Load your bodies with hard works and your minds with duties."

Milarepa

Contents

Early Life

In Milarepa's own words...

I am Milarepa blessed by his (Marpa's) mercy.
My father was Mila Shirab Jhantsan,
My mother was Nyantsa Karjan.
And I was called Tubhaga ("Delightful-to-hear").
Because our merits and virtues were of small account,
And the Cause-Effect Karma of the past spares no one,
My father Mila passed away (too early in his life).
The deceiving goods and belongings of our household
Were plundered by my aunt and uncle,
Whom I and my mother had to serve.
They gave us food fit only for the dogs;
The cold wind pierced our ragged clothing;
Our skin froze and our bodies were benumbed.
Often I was beaten by my uncle,
And endured his cruel punishment.
Hard was it to avoid my aunt's ill temper.
I lived as best as I could, a lowly servant,

And shrugged my shoulders (in bitter resignation).
Misfortunes descended one after the other;
We suffered so, our hearts despaired.
In desperation, I went to Lamas Yundun and Rondunlaga,
From whom I mastered the magic arts of Tu, Ser and Ded
Witnessed by my aunt and uncle, I brought
Great disaster on their villages and kinsmen,
For which, later, I suffered deep remorse.
Then I heard the fame of Marpa, the renowned Translator,
Who, blessed by the saints Naropa and Medripa,
Was living in the upper village of the South River.
After a hard journey I arrived there.
For six years and eight months (I stayed)
With him, my gracious Father Guru, Marpa.
For him I built many houses,
One with courtyards and nine storeys;
Only after this did he accept me.

Then Milarepa lists the meditation instructions, which his
Guru Marpa gave him after he had served a long period of
hard probation, and tells how by their practice he reached
Enlightenment:

I renounced all affairs of this life;
And, no longer lazy, devoted myself to Dharma.
Thus I have reached the State of Eternal Bliss.
Such is the story of my life.

The Story of Tubhaga

Mila Shirab Gyaltsen (Jhantsan), Milarepa's father, married Nyantsa Karjan when he was barely 21 years old. The couple lived happily in the Tibetan village of Kyangatsa in the province of Gungthang (near the border of Nepal).

Mila's family lived in an impressive stone house, called 'The Four Columns and Eight Pillars'. They had considerable land and a thriving business of wool trade. After some time, Mila's brother, Yungdrup Gyaltsen and his wife Khyung Tsha Pedon, also moved into the area. Mila's family helped them to establish a business, to find land and to build a house, and so things went well for these relatives as well.

While Nyantsa Karjan was pregnant with Milarepa, her husband went away on a long trading tour. So during Mila's absence, his baby was born. A messenger was sent to inform him that he had a baby son. He was also asked to give a name to his son. Mila was delighted to hear the news of his son, and named him Tubhaga. 'Tubha' means to hear, and 'ga' means happy or joyous, so his name meant 'a joy to hear'.

Later, as a great mystic (Milarepa), Tubhaga sang wonderful songs, filling the hearts of people with joy.

After some time, Mila returned home and gave a big celebration in honour of his son.

Four years after Tubhaga's birth, a daughter was born into the family and she was called Peta Gonkyi.

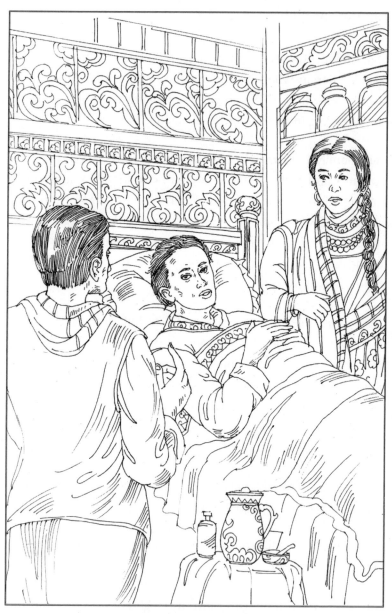

Sick Mila calls his brother and wife

When Tubhaga was seven years old, his father became very sick. Realising that he was not likely to recover from his illness, Mila Shirab Gyaltsen called together all his relatives for a meeting, including Yungdrup Gyaltsen and Khyung Tsha, his brother and his wife.

Mila told them, "I am giving you the responsibility of my lands and all my goods, including my house, because I realise that I will not get over this illness. You must take care of everything until my two children come of age. Please see to it that no harm comes to them; protect them from difficulties, and help them in whatever way you can."

He also said that Zessay, a young girl from the village, had been promised Tubhaga as his future wife through arrangements made with her parents. When Tubhaga was of age, he was to be married to her, and all the property was to be handed over to them. A will was thus written, and signed and sealed. The brother and his wife agreed to carry out these wishes, and having settled his affairs, Mila Shirab Gyaltsen died.

Soon after Mila's death, Tubhaga's uncle and aunt (Mila's brother and his wife) became greedy. They took the money and the land, and everything entrusted to them, and forced Tubhaga, his sister Peta, and their mother, to work as their servants. This went on for nearly seven years.

Nyantsa Karjan, however, had managed to save a little bit of funds, and when Tubhaga was fifteen years old, she invited the people from the village for a meal, including the aunt and the

Tubhaga's mother holds a feast

uncle. She said to the aunt and the uncle, "Tubhaga, is now 15 years old, and it is time for him to get married to Zessay, his fiancée, and to begin his own life. Now please give us back what was entrusted to you by my husband for all these years."

But the greedy aunt and uncle claimed that they had been the original owners and had only loaned the property to her husband and thus, Tubhaga and his mother had no real claim on the property. The aunt and uncle further called them ungrateful wretches, to act like this after accepting the charity of living with them and eating their food! And so, Tubhaga, his mother and sister, were driven out of their own house.

The parents of Tubhaga's fiancée, Zessay, were kind to them, and comforted them, saying that wealth is not permanent, but something that is made by people through their work. They told Tubhaga, "In the beginning your ancestors had no money, but they made it through working. For lack of money, don't be disappointed or discouraged. You must study and develop capabilities, and while you are doing this, whatever you need, will be provided by us."

Tubhaga's teacher from the village was also the local priest, who went around to different houses performing religious ceremonies. Tubhaga accompanied him as an attendant, and on these rounds, they were often given food and drink.

One day when Tubhaga was returning home earlier than his teacher, his mother was on the roof of their house and saw him coming. Tubhaga was a little bit tipsy and was singing a song.

When his mother saw this, she became outraged. Yelling at him in a loud voice, she came tearing down the steps with a stick in her hand, crying, "Tubhaga, you are a child with no father, and you are going around drunk, and singing! While your sister and I are suffering… Your aunt and uncle have taken all our money and cattle, and here you are just wandering around drunk. We had great hopes that you would study and earn some money, yet here you are…"

Tubhaga felt ashamed, and cried, "You are right. I have been behaving terribly, and whatever you say I will gladly do. I had a little bit to drink at the house of a patron, but the song that I sang arose out of sadness. In future I won't drink. Please be patient with me."

His mother said, "I will sell a piece of my ancestral land to get money for your clothes and food. In our family there is a lineage of men who have been powerful in the use of mantra, and so I want you to go to a capable and skilled lama, from whom you should learn how to perform various kinds of magic. Do this; until you can create various signs that everyone can see. It should be obvious that you have magical powers. If you can't do this, I will jump off the roof of the house and kill myself. If you do it, I will offer great prayers for you."

Tubhaga's mother then sent him on his way; giving him her emerald wedding ring and some money that she got by selling a piece of her land.

In his long search for a qualified wizard, Tubhaga met all kinds charlatans, who robbed him of all his assets. At last he arrived in Utsang, the central part of Tibet, where he met lama Yungton Trogyal of Kyorpo, who was a well-known sorcerer of black magic.

Tubhaga told the lama about his mother's vow to kill herself in his presence if he didn't learn some real magic. He then recounted his tale of woes in all its detail to the lama, who was greatly saddened by the story.

Lama Trogyal then suggested, "Since I know only the art of launching hailstorms, you must go to my friend, called, 'Ocean of Talents' of Ku-lung, with my letter. He knows the mantra for causing death and destruction, and will help you."

So Tubhaga went to Ku-lung.

The lama of Ku-lung agreed to confer some power on Tubhaga, and showed him the potent rituals for invoking the Tutelary deities to take revenge.

Tubhaga absorbed all the teachings thoroughly and carefully carried out the prescribed ritual for 14 days. At the end of the ritual the Tutelary deities appeared to him in a vision with the bloody heads and hearts of 35 of the relatives who had ill-treated him the most. The lama informed him that two of the guilty ones had been missed and asked Tubhaga if he wanted their lives as well. Tubhaga replied that he wanted them to be spared as witnesses to the power of his magic.

Back in his village, the aunt and uncle's son was getting married.

Tubhaga causes destruction

They were having a large feast in their house, to which many relatives had been invited.

Using his black magic, Tubhaga summoned a monstrous scorpion – it stuck its claws into the main pillar of the house, pulling it outwards. The horses, in the stables below the house, started kicking and running about violently, agitated, until one of them ran into the main supporting column of the three-storey house with such force that the entire house came crashing down on the wedding party, killing everyone inside except for the aunt and uncle. In all, thirty-five people died.

Tubhaga's mother learned of the catastrophe and was ecstatic with cruel joy. She gloated over the wreck that her son had caused, telling everyone what relief her son had brought to her aging heart by causing so much death and destruction. The relatives of the dead were quite upset at the tragedy and more so to see her gloating. They decided to find and kill the son.

Soon word of their plans got back to the mother and she sent a message to her son, along with some gold pieces she got from selling the rest of her ancestral land. In the note to her son, she described her joy at his success and requested him now to launch a powerful hailstorm on the area, ruining the crops of their enemies and striking fear into their hearts, so as to prevent further retaliation.

Tubhaga received the note and went to Lama Trogyal. He gave the gold pieces to the lama, requesting him to teach him the art of launching hailstorms.

Tubhaga creates hailstorms

In seven days time, armed with his new magic, Tubhaga travelled back to his homeland and set up his ritualistic site on a hillside overlooking the valley of his homeland below. He began his incantations and soon dark clouds began to gather and then a succession of three powerful hailstorms utterly ruined the entire barley crop of that year. At this point the relatives surrendered to the magical power of Tubhaga.

His mother was filled with happiness. She took all the red cloths she had, tied them to the end of a stick, and waving it like a victory banner at the top of the house, she said in a loud voice to the whole village, "The son that was born to Shirab Gyaltsen and myself has come of age. He has given an answer to our enemies and conquered them. Now if there are others in this village who wish to harm us, please come forth!"

No one did.

The Search for the Right Path

Although Tubhaga's mother was delighted with what her son had accomplished, he himself was disappointed. He knew it was wrong to kill and cause such destruction to the crops, and this knowledge worried him. He worried greatly over the heavy debts of karma he had incurred through his evil actions and could think of nothing else.

He wanted to ask Lama Trogyal for religious instruction but did not have the courage to broach the subject, so he stayed on, faithfully serving the lama and waiting for an opportune moment to bring up the subject of his salvation.

Once the lama was called away to attend to one of his followers who had died after a short illness. The lama returned lamenting that such an excellent man in the prime of his life had died so suddenly. He spoke on the transitory nature of life and the misery of this earthly existence and then started ruminating over his own life.

Lama Trogyal said, "All created things are impermanent. Through practising magic and making hail, I have been able to accumulate a bit of wealth in this life but this will be of little help when I die. The only thing that can help us is the practise of Dharma, and that is what I would like to do. But I am old now and it is difficult to practise; yet since there is no other way to liberate myself from the evil consequences of my deeds, I must do it. You, on the other hand, are not as old as me. You have a lot of energy and diligence and could practise genuine Dharma. Doing this, you would be able to attain Buddhahood. You could then liberate the souls of all the beings we have killed."

In this mood of deep remorse, he urged Tubhaga to go and seek out Lama Rongton Lhaga to learn the doctrine of 'The Great Perfection,' and deliver himself into a higher state of existence in a future life. This was the opportunity Tubhaga had been waiting for.

Tubhaga then went to the western part of central Tibet, to Lama Rongton Lhaga. Having bowed to him, he said, "I have committed great negative actions. I have tremendous fear of Samsaara; therefore, please teach me the Dharma that will allow me to liberate myself in this life."

The lama replied, "If you can practise from the depths of your being, if you can totally involve yourself in this practice, then if you meditate for one day, this Dharma of the Great Perfection that I teach will bring liberation in one day. For fortunate beings, merely hearing this Dharma will bring liberation."

Tubhaga thought he must be one of the fortunate beings who, once they hear such a teaching would be able to realise liberation in one life. 'If in only some days of studying and practice, I was able to achieve the magical powers that allowed me to destroy the house and produce hail, as no one else was able to, I am sure I can accomplish this practice in a shorter time. All you have to do is hear it and your mind becomes happy. I have heard this, and I feel pretty happy.' Thinking in this way, Tubhaga went and slept for seven days.

A week later, the lama came and enquired, "What kind of experiences did you have? What kind of realisations arose?"

Tubhaga replied, "My mind is most peaceful and happy. I have had a fine time sleeping here."

The lama replied, "I probably gave you this teaching a bit too early. You are someone who has accumulated a lot of negative actions, and although this teaching has great qualities, I am not the one who will be able to train you. You should go to a country called Drowolung, in southern Tibet where 'Marpa the Translator' lives. He is skilled in the secret mantrayana. You should go and study with him."

When Tubhaga heard the name of Marpa, an inexpressible feeling of joy arose within him. He set out on the road to Marpa's house and came to a place called Dharma Ridge, where he saw some children playing. A man, who was covered with the dust of the road, stood nearby. Tubhaga asked him, "Where is the house of the King of Translators, Marpa?" The man replied, "I don't know who the King of Translators is, but a Marpa lives over there." He pointed down the road, which Tubhaga followed.

The night before Tubhaga arrived at Marpa's house, Marpa's wife Dagmema had a dream in which Naropa presented a crystal sceptre, slightly soiled, and a golden vase with water to Marpa. With the water from the golden vase, Marpa purified the crystal sceptre and placed it on the peak of a mountain. From this peak, luminous rays of the sun and the moon filled the cosmos.

That same night, a dream came to Marpa as well, in which Naropa appeared and gave Marpa a five-pointed lapis lazuli sceptre, which also had some dirt on it, and along with it, a vase of water. With the water of that vase, the stains were washed away from the lapis lazuli sceptre, and it was placed on top of a victory banner from whence light radiated to the whole world.

When Dagmema brought Marpa his morning tea, they told each other of their dreams. From the dream Marpa knew that a momentous meeting with his chief disciple was about to take place and that his task was to remove some evil karma by which the disciple had been tarnished and then to bring him to the state of enlightenment. He told so to his wife, and asked her to get some good *chang* (a drink made with barley).

Marpa then left his house, telling his wife that he was going to plough his field that day, a thing he had never done before. Marpa went to the field, keeping a sharp eye out for whoever was coming along the road.

Tubhaga was walking along the road and came upon a group of children playing. Among them was a child who seemed well cared for. This was Dharma Dode, Marpa's son. Tubhaga asked

Tubhaga sees Marpa ploughing

this young child, "I am looking for the King of Translators, Marpa, who is supposed to live in this area."

The child replied, "You are probably looking for my father," and pointed him the direction of his house. Tubhaga walked along the path and came to a field where someone was ploughing. This person had a well filled-out body, with a certain brilliance radiating from his face. The field was all ploughed, but for a small part that was not yet finished.

As soon as Tubhaga saw this person, he was filled with such an inexpressible bliss that he was unable to speak for a while. When words came, Tubhaga asked, "Do you know where the house of the King of Translators, Marpa, is?"

Marpa took a long, slow look at him from head to foot, and said, "Stay here. Drink this *chang*, plough the field, and I will introduce you to Marpa."

Tubhaga did as he was told. Shortly, the child whom he had met before, came to him and said, "Follow me. The lama has asked for you."

Tubhaga did not leave right away but finished ploughing the field and then went to Marpa's house. There, Tubhaga found, sitting on two cushions covered with a rug, the same man who was ploughing the field. Marpa said to him, "I am Marpa."

Tubhaga prostrated before him and said, "I am a great sinner who has committed tremendous negative actions. I offer you, however, my body, speech, and mind. Please give me food, clothing, and the teachings of Dharma so that I can attain Buddhahood in this very life."

Marpa replied, "It does not really concern me that you have committed negative actions. What is important is that you have offered me your body, speech, and mind. Now as for food, clothing and Dharma: If I give you Dharma, you will have to get your food and clothing elsewhere. If I give you food and clothing, you will have to get your Dharma elsewhere. So this depends on you."

Tubhaga decided to receive Dharma from Marpa and to find his own food and clothing. In order to gather the latter, Tubhaga had to go to the local village. By begging, he amassed twenty-one measures of wheat, fourteen of which he used to buy a large copper pot with four handles. When he returned to Marpa's house, Tubhaga was very relieved and quickly let his burden drop onto the floor of the house. It shook.

Marpa left the meal he was eating to come and speak to Tubhaga, "Young man, you are very strong. Dropping this load of grain you carried has shaken the whole house. Perhaps you are getting ready to kill me. (Marpa was recalling Tubhaga's black magic that had caused his aunt and uncle's house to collapse and kill many people.) Don't leave this grain here. Take it out!"

Tubhaga thought that Marpa was a little short-tempered, as he took his sack of grain outside and left it there. He then offered Marpa the copper pot with the four handles, saying, "Please give me the secret instructions that will allow me to free myself from suffering in this lifetime."

Marpa lifted up the cooper pot and said, "I offer this to the great master Naropa." Tears came to his eyes and he made a prophecy, "You gave me an empty pot – this means that in this life while you are practising in retreat, you may have a bit of difficulty with food; but when I hit the pot, it gave off a wonderfully resonant sound. This is a sign that you will become very famous. The four handles facing the four directions, are a sign, that I will have great spiritual sons." (Tubhaga, as Milarepa, would be one of them.)

Finally, Marpa filled the copper pot with clarified butter and inserted many wicks in it, so that it glowed with the warm light. In the future, this copper pot would be placed within a great stupa, he said.

In response to Tubhaga's request for the Dharma, Marpa replied, "I have heard that you killed a number of people with your magic by sending hail. Is this true or not?" Tubhaga had to admit that it was true.

Marpa then told him, "In the village behind you, there is a place where my students must pass when they come to see me and the villagers treat them terribly. They beat them, they steal from them, and sometimes they don't even let them through. I want you to go there and send hail onto this village. If you can do it, there is no way that I would not be able to give you this precious, profound lineage of Naropa I have received with such hardship."

Tubhaga walked to the village and spoke to the people there, telling them how poorly they had treated Marpa's students and that there was no reason for this. He berated them severely and they responded with anger, attacking and beating him. As they were ready to kick him out of town, Tubhaga said, "You've made problems for the lama and his students, and now I will make trouble for you. Through my magic, I will send a powerful sign to you. It will not be pleasant!" Tubhaga left to perform his magic, and this time the result was to make the villagers fight, beating and knocking each other down. They finally realised that this was the result of Tubhaga's magic, so they came to see Marpa and apologised. They promised not to hurt his disciples as they came through the village. After this, Marpa gave Tubhaga a new name, 'Great Magician'.

Having fulfilled this task for Marpa, Tubhaga again asked for the teachings. Marpa said, "There is another place a little bit distant from here, where they also give my students a difficult time. Go and send hail on their harvest. And then once you have done that, I will give you the teachings."

With the thought that in accomplishing the commands of the lama he would obtain Buddhahood in this life, Tubhaga left for this second village. When he came to the countryside nearby, he stayed with an old woman. The harvest was growing very well and crops were flourishing. Tubhaga told the old woman that he was going to send hail and it would not only destroy the crops but also, when the hail melted, carry away the topsoil. The old woman was upset at the thought of losing her land and harvest.

Tubhaga suggested that she draw a picture of her land. He took a metal pot and covered the part of the map that was the old woman's land except for a little piece of it. He then performed his magic and the hail came. The harvest was destroyed and the topsoil was carried away, except for the small piece of land that belonged to the old lady. The small portion that was not covered by the pot was also carried away, but all that was covered was saved, while the rest of the village was devastated.

The villagers were stunned and surprised that everything was destroyed except for the old woman's land. They came to speak with her, "Why is it that your land was not destroyed?" She replied, "I kept by me a young monk who was very clever. I gave him food and lodging. You should ask him."

They went to Tubhaga. Why did this happen? They asked. He answered, "You have made a lot of trouble for the students of my lama, Marpa. If you go to him and confess, then in the future such things will not happen." So they went to Marpa and confessed, promising not to harm his disciples.

But later, thinking about what he had done, Tubhaga became depressed and discouraged. In the past he had killed human beings and he now realised that in sending hail he had killed a lot of small sentient beings as well. "If I think of the causes and conditions for rebirth in a future life, I have killed many people, and now I have killed small sentient beings as well. I will certainly be born in the hell realms."

He went to Marpa and begged him, "My negative activity is

increasing and certainly in the next life I will be born in a burning hot hell. Please, through your great compassion grant me the teachings of the Dharma."

Marpa said, "Indeed you have committed many negative actions and the antidote for the karma you have accumulated is Dharma. However, if you think right now you are ready to get the precious Dharma for which I had to accumulate much gold to offer Naropa, and then travel along the hazardous route to India; if you think you are ready to get this now, you are overstepping yourself. Whatever work I have set out for you, you have done earnestly and well; however, in order to receive my Dharma, you must be someone who is willing to put his whole heart into it. Only that kind of person can truly receive my Dharma. Now I am going to test you to see if you have that kind of heart. I want you to build a house for my son Dharma Dode. Once you have completed the house, I will give you the Dharma, and not only will I give you the Dharma, I will give you food and clothing as well."

Tubhaga asked, "What happens if I die building this house before I can receive the Dharma?" Marpa promised, "I guarantee you will not die building this house. You will receive the Dharma."

Serving the Master

Not far from where Marpa lived, there was some land in the middle of a village. The local people had all agreed that no one would own this land and it would be held in common. They had all signed a paper to this effect, except for Marpa, because he wanted to build a house there for his son. But he had to be clever about it. If he just went there and built it, the villagers would protest, so he had Tubhaga do the job.

Marpa made Tubhaga first build a round house in the eastern direction. When Tubhaga had half finished it, Marpa said, "I don't think this has turned out very well." He told Tubhaga to tear it down, return all the stones to the place from where he had taken them, and all the earth back to the holes from where he had dug it. So Tubhaga returned all the stones to their place, all the earth to where it belonged, and then went back to Marpa, "I have followed all your commands, now please teach me the Dharma."

Marpa replied, "It is not quite time yet. I want you to build a house in the shape of a half circle, overlooking the south. Once you have finished building it, I will teach you the Dharma." Tubhaga again went out and started collecting stones and earth and began to build up the walls of the second house. When he had progressed considerably, Marpa came to see him, "Who told you to build this house?" Tubhaga said, "You did!" Marpa replied, "I must have been drunk or crazy. I don't remember anything about telling you to build this house." So Tubhaga again had to take down the house and return all the stones and all the earth back to their places. Having completed the task, Tubhaga went back to Marpa and said, "I have finished all the work you told me to do. Please grant me the teachings of Dharma."

Marpa said to him, "Now in the future you shouldn't be doing work that you weren't told to do. Actually what really needs to be built is a triangular-shaped building, in the western direction. If you finish this house, I will teach you the Dharma, and not only that, I will celebrate it with a great feast."

This time Tubhaga was a little anxious, "Precious lama, the first time you said you hadn't thought it through very well, it wasn't what you really wanted, and the next time you said you really didn't remember having told me to build that house. Now again you are telling me to build a triangular-shaped house. Would you mind if I brought in your wife as a witness to this?" Marpa agreed that his wife Dagmema could be the witness. Dagmema said, "I am not really sure what the reason is behind all this work he has given you, but if it is done for the sake of the Dharma, then I will be a witness."

Again, Tubhaga went to gather together earth and rocks to make a house, and slowly the walls of the house were built up. It was such heavy work however, that large sores began to appear on his back. Since he could no longer carry things on his back, he carried them on his hip, but then sores also developed there, and so he carried things on his chest and sores developed there. He was full of sores, and not only that, the water and earth he was carrying to make mortar, entered into them and it was very painful for him. Yet he thought, this was the command of his lama, and continued his work with diligence.

Though he was in much pain, Tubhaga reflected, "I can't really show these sores or speak of these problems to Marpa because he would probably get angry with me. His wife is full of compassion and kindness, but if I show them to her, she would probably think I am proud of all the work I've done." With no place to turn, he was filled with despair.

Dagmema found him weeping and asked him the reason, but Tubhaga did not reply. She said, "Don't cry; you will get the Dharma teaching." Tubhaga finally told her his real feelings; "You are kind to me as a mother. And in order to obtain the precious Dharma, I must build this house. Yet in building this house my body is becoming nothing but a huge wound. Until now I worked as hard as I could, carrying stones and earth, but it has become extremely painful."

Dagmema looked at Tubhaga's body, which had been covered before, and seeing all his festering, open sores, she cried, "You are right. I've never seen such wounds on a human being before.

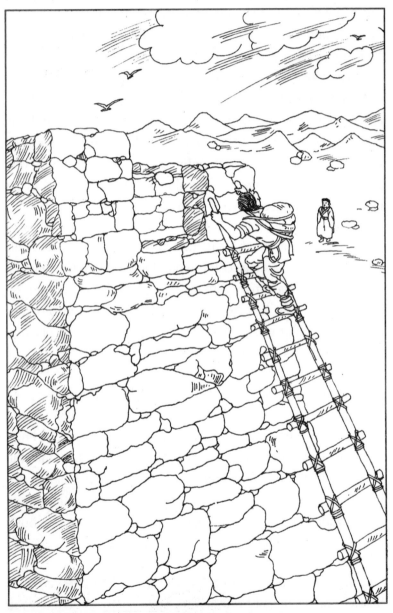

Tubhaga builds a house for Marpa

Your situation is even worse than an animal's. A horse only gets saddle sores on its back, but you have them all over your body. I don't understand why Marpa is making you go through all of this. But stay here and I will take care of you. I will go to Marpa on your behalf and try to see if I can arrange for you to receive the Dharma."

Dagmema went to Marpa, and described to him what Tubhaga was going through, and Marpa also cried, "Such diligence and great effort made for the sake of Dharma, and to fulfill the commands of the lama, makes me very happy."

Marpa agreed that until Tubhaga's wounds were healed, he could stay; Dagmema could give him good food and bring him back to health. She took good care of him and Tubhaga was happy. His mind, however, was not satisfied; he had not yet received the Dharma.

One day Marpa was giving the initiation of Chakrasamvara (Demchok). Many of his students had come and brought wonderful offerings. Tubhaga also went and happily joined the crowd. But Marpa looked at him and asked, "What do you have to offer?" Tubhaga replied, "Well, I've been building this house and that's my offering." Marpa admonished him, "You're building this house, but it's not finished. It's a finished house that you must offer." And he chased Tubhaga away.

Tubhaga went to Dagmema, who comforted him, "Don't worry. Slowly, with time, you will receive the Dharma."

After the initiation ceremony, Marpa came to Tubhaga and asked, "We had a little bit of argument the other day. Has your mind not turned against me for this?" Tubhaga replied, "I have committed monstrous negative actions. They are the cause of the bad things that happen to me. My faith in the lama has not changed, not at all." Marpa said, "That's good. I went through great difficulties in order to bring the Dharma from India. So now, you go back and finish building the walls."

One day, Marpa came to Tubhaga, who was in the process of building the triangular-shaped house. "Great Magician, who told you to build this house?" he asked. "Lama, you were the one who told me to build this house!" answered Tubhaga.

Marpa retorted, "This is a triangular-shaped house. Triangular-shaped houses are for evil magicians who use mantra in their practices. What are you doing? Planning on staying here and performing black magic on me? Are you going to kill me?" And commanded that he tear down this magician's palace and replace the stones where they came from and carry the earth back to its place.

Once more Tubhaga returned and reported to Marpa that he had fulfilled his command. Marpa replied, "Well, what do you need then?" "I need the Dharma. Please give me the Dharma," begged Tubhaga. Marpa finally agreed and told Dagmema to make a good meal and give it to Tubhaga. Then Marpa gave him refuge vows and advice. He also gave him the short spiritual biography of Naropa that describes the twelve difficulties he had to go through. Marpa said to Tubhaga, "I have given you now what is called the common or general Dharma. As I said, if you want the uncommon or exceptional Dharma, you must have the capacity to go through extreme difficulties to demonstrate faith in the lama and to maintain stable, unchanging samaya. Is this something you can do?"

The fourth house that Tubhaga was asked to build was to become the famous nine-storied tower called Se Kar Gu Tok, 'the house with nine storeys for the son'. Marpa had drawn the plan for it on the ground, and Tubhaga had started the construction. As the tower was located on the land of the village where no one was supposed to build, the people became concerned, 'What's going to happen with this house that's going up on our land?' Some thought, 'Well, maybe Marpa won't really build it. He's started all these other houses and they've come down.' Other people said, 'Well, he's just crazy. He's having all these houses put up by this student who's real strong. Three-cornered houses and four-cornered houses, and they're just going up and down and this one is going to come down, too, just like the rest of them.' And then they said, 'If he doesn't destroy this house, then we'll gather together and fight him. We'll bring it down ourselves.'

The nine-storey tower was built all the way up to the top. Tubhaga built it all by himself, with not even one stone being carried by another person. He went through untold physical hardship. By the end, the only thing missing was the roof. At last when the villagers realised that this one was not going to be destroyed, they got together and decided to attack it.

Realising what was happening, Marpa created an illusory army that circled the tower in all directions preventing anyone from coming close. The villagers were astounded. Seeing they were up against a force beyond their strength, they went to Marpa, apologised, and promised that they would not destroy the tower.

During the long and difficult period of the tower construction, no matter what Tubhaga did, Marpa would never give him the teachings. Tubhaga finally despaired, "It looks as if I'm not going to get Dharma teachings from Marpa. I will have to go to another lama." He went to Dagmema, and explained his thoughts to her. She consoled him, "Well, it's all right. You're not to blame for this. The lama's very difficult, and he's given you a tough time. Keep working on the house, and I will work something out so that you can receive Dharma teachings."

One day, Dagmema wrote a letter making it seem as if it came from Marpa, to one of his main disciples, Lama Ngogpa. It read, "I'm extremely busy. There are too many students, and I can't give teaching to this Great Magician. Please, give him some Dharma teachings."

There was a festival coming up, a grand celebration, and Dagmema had made some strong chang, which she gave to Marpa during the ceremonies. He got quite drunk and she was able to take his seal and stamp the letter. Then Dagmema took a ruby rosary that had belonged to Naropa and also some bone ornaments that had belonged to him.

Giving the letter, the ruby rosary, and the bones to Tubhaga, Dagmema said, "Here, take these blessed objects and this letter, but don't say I'm the one who gave them to you. Pretend they are from Marpa and that you are one of his disciples. Take these to Lama Ngogpa. I will say prayers for you. Practise diligently. Don't have any wrong views about Marpa. I have great hope that you will indeed receive teachings from him eventually." She gave him some food and sent him on his way.

When Tubhaga reached, Lama Ngogpa was sitting on a high throne teaching hundreds of students. As Tubhaga approached him, he was reciting these lines, "I am the one who explains, I am the Dharma that is explained, and I am those who have gathered to hear the teachings. I am the guide of the world and the one who creates the world. I am of the world and beyond it. I am the true nature of spontaneous bliss." In Tibetan tradition, the point at which teachings are interrupted by such an event are considered very significant.

Tubhaga bowed to Lama Ngogpa from a distance. The lama stood up on his high throne, took off his hat, and bowed in response to Tubhaga's prostrations. The students were surprised and asked their lama, "Who is this that you're treating with such respect?" Lama Ngogpa replied, "Ask him who he is. His way of prostrating is like that of Marpa, so I assumed he was his disciple and bowed to him." One of the students approached and questioned Tubhaga, who responded as Dagmema had told him – he lied. He said that he was a student of Marpa's, that he had come to take Dharma teachings from Lama Ngogpa, that Marpa had sent him, and that he had brought a ruby rosary and bone ornaments from Naropa as confirmation.

When Lama Ngogpa heard this, he was extremely happy. "Wonderful! Tell him not to come right away, but to wait." The students told Tubhaga that they were going to form a great procession for him in the traditional style with victory banners, music, and the monks wearing all their fine robes. Tubhaga was asked to wait until they could receive him properly. He was exuberant. With all the brilliant ceremony, he thought he had arrived in the land of the gods and now at least he was going to receive the teaching. He felt this was all due to the kindness of Dagmema and shed tears remembering her.

Lama Ngogpa gave Tubhaga teachings and also taught him how to practise. Tubhaga meditated for quite a while, but nothing happened – nothing at all. There were no signs of realisation, no experiences, nothing. Lama Ngogpa was astounded. With these teachings, there was no way that nothing could happen. What was going on? He began to have some doubts, so he questioned Tubhaga more closely, and finally Tubhaga told the truth – that the letter wasn't from Marpa and neither was the rosary or the bone ornaments. Lama Ngogpa said, "Well, that must be the truth, because without the lama's blessings, experience and realisation cannot arise."

About this time, a letter arrived for Lama Ngogpa from Marpa. It read, "The house is finally finished and I'm going to have a big celebration in honour of this occasion. Please come with your students and bring whatever you have to offer. As for that lousy student of mine, you can bring him along, too."

Except for one goat with a bad leg, which he thought wasn't good enough to offer and thus left at home, Lama Ngogpa took everything he had gathered throughout his life, as an offering to Marpa.

As they approached Marpa's house, Lama Ngogpa felt a little tired, it having been a long journey, and so he said to Tubhaga, "You go on ahead, and from the house bring me out some *chang* to drink. Before we get there, I'd like to just rest a little bit." Tubhaga went to the house and met Dagmema, who was delighted to see him. He delivered Lama Ngogpa's message and Dagmema said, "Fine, but first we should go and greet Marpa."

Tubhaga explained to Marpa that Lama Ngogpa had come, that he was a little tired from the journey and that he would like some *chang*. Marpa became furious, "What! I went to India at the risk of my life to get this Dharma teaching from Naropa. No one was there to greet me with *chang*. What's this person talking about? If he wants *chang*, he can come to the house."

Soon, the party arrived at Marpa's house. Lama Ngogpa then said to Marpa, "I give you power over my body, speech, and mind, and all the wealth that I have. Whatever I possess, I offer to you. The only thing I haven't offered you is one goat with a bad leg. I ask you to give me the special instructions of the Dakinis." Marpa replied, "All the other Dharma I know I have given you, but if you want to receive this secret instruction of the Dakinis, you'll have to bring me that goat."

Lama Ngogpa went back to his house and fetched the goat. It took him one day to return to his house, and then he walked the whole night back with the goat on his shoulders and offered it to Marpa.

PART IV

Empowerment and Attainment

Marpa was very happy, "In order for you to receive these teachings, I really didn't need this goat. However, there was a purpose in your going to get it. You demonstrated great respect for these teachings, and showed that you're the proper kind of student. Whatever kind of difficulty you're given, you're able to carry through. This shows the strength of your devotion."

Lama Ngogpa and all his students assembled for the empowerment, and yet again Tubhaga was not allowed to attend. At this point, he was totally depressed. Extremely disappointed, he said, "I'm going to jump in the river. I'm going to end it all. This is more than I can take." As he lifted up his things to put them on his back, he reflected that this indeed was a human body he had attained, despite having done a lot of negative things; moreover, in the future it wasn't certain that he would again attain a human body and meet a real lama. So again, he decided to stay but remained in a very distressed state of mind.

Through his omniscient knowledge, Marpa knew what was happening within Tubhaga's mind. Dagmema came before him and said, "Through all these hardships, this wonderful student of yours has neither rejected you nor the Dharma. Not once has he turned his mind away from the Dharma no matter how difficult it was." She begged Marpa to give him the teachings. Marpa finally assented and told Lama Ngogpa and his students to fill the shrine with abundant offerings, for that day the guest of honour would be Tubhaga.

First they made a place for Tubhaga to sit. Then Marpa briefly gave him a teaching on the Dharma in general, which included fulfilling the commands of the teacher and undergoing hardships for the sake of the Dharma. During the initiation of Chakrasamvara, Tubhaga experienced the face of the yidam deity. Marpa held up a kapala (skull cup) filled with amrita, which functioned as a support for visualisation. He dipped his index finger in the amrita and told Tubhaga to look at it with great faith. In the sky in front of him, Tubhaga saw the full mandala of Chakrasamvara – the main deity and the retinue with all the offerings.

In complete unity with the deity Chakrasamvara, Marpa made a prophesy about Tubhaga based on the empty copper pot with four handles that Tubhaga had given him when he first came. The four handles represented the four main heart sons of Marpa, of which Tubhaga was one. The fact that the pot was empty meant that he was going to have some problems with food during his practice in this life, but Marpa had filled it with melted butter and this meant that, in the future, his lineage would be fruitful. He would have many excellent students and through them, the Buddha's teaching would spread widely. Gods and men would sing praises to Tubhaga and he would be able to prolong his life through the practice of samadhi.

Above in the sky, all the gods were happy. Below the earth, all the nagas were happy. And in between, in the realm of human beings, everyone was happy.

After receiving initiation into the lineage of the deity, and the secret oral instructions for the practice, Tubhaga began his formal practice by going into retreat for eleven months. Balancing a full butter lamp on top of his head, he stayed in a cave that was walled in. Day and night he practised in this way. At the end of the eleven months, Marpa and Dagmema came to see him.

Tubhaga had been inside the cave for so long, he was hesitant to come out. He didn't feel he could break down the wall himself. Dagmema helped to break down the wall and Tubhaga emerged, made prostrations to Marpa and received his blessings.

Tubhaga was then led into the circle of disciples. Marpa gave Tubhaga a kapala full of amrita, and Tubhaga drank it all. Then, together with all the disciples, Marpa gave teachings on the nature of the mind. In addition, he bestowed initiations of various yidam deities, which matured the vajra body, speech, and mind of Tubhaga. (It was these yidam deities who gave Tubhaga the name Zhepa Dorje, the Laughing Vajra.)

There were many auspicious signs at the time, such as flowers falling from the sky. Marpa and Dagmema gave Tubhaga another name: Mila Dorje Gyaltsen, Vajra Victory Banner.

After the initiations, Marpa gathered all the students around him and addressed Tubhaga, "Great Magician, you are my karmically connected son. I knew this from the very beginning. When I was ploughing the field – that was my way of going out to meet you. However, you had killed many people and other sentient beings. In order to purify these negative actions, you had to go through all the trials. Eight times you were thrown into despair. All these occasions were to purify negative actions, to make stronger your renunciation of Samsaara. Now, during this time, my wife, Dagmema, who has great compassion, was very kind to you. She gave you food and comforted you again and again, but this made for an imperfect situation. She did not challenge you enough, and, therefore, not all of your negative actions have been purified. You must go to a solitary place in the mountains and practise in retreat to slowly purify yourself of these negative actions. Although you went through great difficulties, never did you have wrong views, either about Dharma or myself. This is wonderful: due to this circumstance, in the future your students will be genuine practitioners. They will also have faith and will not generate any negative views."

Marpa continued, "The view and the practice of Dharma that I teach is extremely important, wondrous, and most unusual, because within the secret Vajrayana, there's a special link between the lama and the student. Whatever happens between the two of them happens in order to develop the qualities of the student. If anger arises, it's not a normal arising of anger. There is a purpose to it. All of the Dharma teachings that I brought back from India at the risk of my life, I will give to you. But first, since you have stayed eleven months in retreat, please tell us what kind of experience and what kind of realisation you have attained."

Tubhaga first sang a song which he extemporaneously composed honouring his teacher and his wife, and the teachings he had been given. In his song he requested that Marpa remain in the world until 'The Whirling Pool of Being is emptied'. After that he summarized his realisations.

- I have understood this body of mine to be the product of ignorance, composed of flesh and blood and lit up by the perceptive power of consciousness. To those fortunate ones who long for emancipation it may be the great vessel by which they may procure Freedom. But to the unfortunates who only sin, it may be the guide to lower and miserable states of existence. This our life is the boundary mark whence one may take an upward or downward path. Our present time is a most precious time, wherein each of us must decide, in one way or other, for lasting good or lasting ill.
- One who aims only at his own individual peace and happiness adopts the lower path (Hinayana), but he who devotes the merits of his love and compassion to the cause of others belongs to the higher path (Mahayana).
- In meditating on the Final Goal, one has to discover the non-existence of the personal Ego, and therefore the fallacy that it exists (i.e. because everything in the universe with name and form is basically illusory in nature)

- To realise the state of non-existence of the personal ego, the mind must be kept in quiescence. In that state, thoughts, ideas, and cognition cease and the mind (awareness) passes into a state of perfect tranquility so that days, months, and years may pass without the person perceiving it; thus the passage of time has to be marked for him by others.

- The visions of the forms of the Deities which appear in meditation are merely signs attending the perseverance in meditation. They have no intrinsic worth or value in themselves.

- All the efforts put forth during this path must be made in a spirit of compassion with the aim of dedicating the merit of one's efforts to the Universal Good. There is a need of mentally praying and wishing for blessings on others so earnestly that one's mind processes also transcend thought.

- Just as the mere name of food does not satisfy the appetite of a hungry person but he must eat food, so also a man who would learn about the Voidness (i.e. Universal Awareness) must meditate so as to realise it, not just learn of its definition.

Marpa was extremely happy with Tubhaga's account. "This is most excellent. You are truly a karmically connected, strong student. And in the future I will give you progressively all the oral instructions, and you must then give yourself fully to these practices."

After celebrating Tubhaga's emergence from the retreat, Marpa gave him more instructions for his next meditation practice. Not long into the next retreat, though, a blue dakini with golden hair, eyebrows, and eyelashes appeared to Tubhaga in a dream. She said to him, "Practicing the Six Yogas of Naropa is very good. However, there is one teaching that has not been obtained. It's called 'The Instantaneous Attainment of Enlightenment.' It is a kind of powa practice enabling you to send your consciousness into another body after you die. You must go ask for this." Having given this advice, she disappeared.

Tubhaga then broke down the wall of his cave and went to Marpa, who was astounded to see him. "I just put you in retreat, what are you doing here? Why did you come out so quickly? Isn't this an obstacle to your practice?" Tubhaga explained to him that a dakini had appeared to him and told him that this teaching of powa had not been received and that it should be asked for.

Marpa said, "When I was with Naropa, he did speak of this kind of powa practice, but I really don't remember whether I have received the teachings or not." So they pulled out all the texts that Marpa had brought back from India, and spent days going through them looking for the teaching, but they could not find it.

Marpa again undertook the arduous journey to India to meet Naropa. Marpa did not find him in his usual place, as Naropa had become a realised siddha, and moved freely. After a long search, he found him, and together they went to Pullahari, north of Bodh Gaya, where Naropa had a place of retreat. It was there that Marpa asked Naropa for the powa instructions. Naropa asked, "Is this something coming from you yourself? Did you want to receive this, or is this something that a yidam deity told you to request?" And Marpa said, "No, it isn't from me. I did not receive this from a yidam. It was my student."

"Good News!" Naropa put his palms together and, bowing towards Tibet, said,

"In the thick darkness of the north, like the sun glistening on the snow, there is one called Good News; it is to this one that I bow."

It is said that at Pullahari, all the trees around the retreat hut of Naropa remain bowing towards Tibet. Naropa also gave Marpa many other teachings, including the Whispered Lineage of the Dakinis. He prophesied that, in the future, the Dharma lineage of Marpa would be masters of this practice, and that his Dharma descendants would maintain his lineage and practise it well.

When Naropa had finished giving him these teachings, Marpa emerged from the hut, and once outside, he bowed again to Naropa. (This was the last time he met him.) As Marpa was making his bows, he left a footprint in the rock that is still visible.

Marpa returned to Tibet, and gave Tubhaga, his main disciple, every single initiation that he had received, including the Whispered Instructions of the Dakini lineage.

There were, however, other disciples of Naropa who received different teachings, and Marpa encouraged Tubhaga and his other students to go and meet them in order to obtain the remaining instructions. In this way, Marpa's students would maintain Naropa's lineage.

After some years, Marpa called all of his students together. He said, "We are maintaining the lineage of Naropa, and we should now look into the future to see what will happen to this lineage. Tonight, watch your dreams carefully, and in the morning, let me know what you've seen."

Tubhaga dreamt of four great pillars, one in each direction. In the eastern direction was Tsurton Wangye, one of the four main disciples. The snow lion on top of his pillar signified that he had a heart like a lion. In the southern direction was Lama Ngogpa, to whom Dagmema had sent Tubhaga for teaching. On top of this pillar was a tiger, symbolising the character of Lama Ngogpa. In the western direction was Meton of Tsangrong, and his symbol was the garuda. On the northern pillar was a vulture, and this represented Tubhaga.

In Tibet, the vulture is considered a being who can endure all kinds of hardship. Vultures also come to eat the bodies that are offered at the cemeteries. They can even eat the bones, which indicates that they have a lot of fire in their bodies that allows them to digest anything.

Tubhaga's specialty was the practice of Tum-mo, which is related to fire. In the dream, the vulture's feathers were all in place and they were beautiful with no fault whatsoever. This was a sign that all of the instructions Tubhaga received would abide within his mindstream and he would remember them perfectly. The vulture's nest is usually high up on the rocks, and this was a sign that Tubhaga would have a long life. Tubhaga also dreamed that the vulture had many offsprings, and that was a sign that Tubhaga would have incomparable disciples. Flying around the vulture in the sky were many different kinds of birds. This was a sign that the Kagyu teachings would increase and spread. The vulture's eyes looked upward into the sky, signifying that Tubhaga had cut his ties to Samsaara and that in the future, he would not need to take physical birth. At the end of the dream, the vulture flew into the sky, showing that Tubhaga would reach the expanse of liberation, or the level of Buddhahood.

After interpreting the dream, Marpa said, "I have explained all this to you and my work now is finished. It's your turn, my disciples, to do the work. And if my words are not false, but true; and if they have the strength to endure, then in the future, this lineage will flourish."

Marpa then gave to each his disciples texts that would be most valuable according to each person's line of development. Each also received some relic that had belonged to Naropa. To Milarepa was given the teaching of Tum-mo in which the ascending and descending flows along the spinal column are united to produce the vital heat so necessary for meditation in the cold and solitary caves of the Himalayas.

While Marpa was in India, Naropa had also prophesied to him that Tubhaga should go back into retreat and pointed out a particular cave. Following these instructions, Tubhaga went back into retreat, with the continuing support of Marpa and Dagmema.

Usually Tubhaga never slept but meditated continuously, however one particular day he had slept for a long time and had a vivid dream wherein he saw the house he had lived in as a child was in ruins. He saw his sacred books within the fallen house being wasted by rainwater, his old mother had died, and his sister was roaming about the countryside alone. In his dream he was weeping with great sadness and longing for his mother and sister and he woke up feeling very sad. He tried again to meditate but could not shed his sadness; instead the feeling grew stronger and stronger until he vowed to himself to go out into the world and try to find his family. So he went to see his guru, Marpa.

As he entered Marpa's quarters he found him asleep with the rising sun just lighting his head like a halo. Just at that moment, Dagmema came in with his morning tea and Marpa woke up.

Tubhaga explained that he was overcome with sadness thinking of his mother and sister he had left behind many years ago. He explained to Marpa his great longing to see them once more. Although Marpa felt there was little chance of finding the mother alive and little merit in making the search, he agreed to allow him to go. But, he warned, the fact that Tubhaga had entered his quarters and found him asleep was an omen that they would not see each other alive again in this life.

Marpa was much grieved thinking he would not see his spiritual son again, but knowing this was the way of all the perishable

Marpa initiates Tubhaga

things of the world, he requested Dagmema to deck the alter with offerings for their parting ceremony. He then gave Tubhaga the final and highest initiation as well as the sacred ear-whispered tantric doctrines. These doctrines he gave only to Tubhaga, among all his disciples. He instructed Tubhaga in his turn to hand them down to his most worthy disciple and so on for thirteen generations.

Then in a final ceremony with the entire assembly of lamas and disciples, Marpa manifested himself in the forms of Gaypa Dorje and other of the tutelary divinities of the Kagyu sect and also other divine shapes and forms along with the various symbols associated with each deity such as bells, gems, lotuses, swords, etc. He then explained that these were various psycho-physical powers obtained after enlightenment and that they should never be manifested for an unworthy cause.

Tubhaga felt greatly exalted to see that his Guru Marpa was veritably a Buddha himself. He vowed that he himself would gain such powers and show in his turn to his own disciples.

Marpa then told him that he could now depart since he had demonstrated the mirage like nature of all existing things. He instructed Tubhaga to meditate in various caves made holy by previous saints in the locales of Mount Kailas, Lapchi Kang (Mt. Everest), and other sanctified places. He then gave to Tubhaga a sealed scroll that was to be opened only on dire threat of imminent death.

With great sadness, knowing they would not meet again in the present life, Tubhaga took leave of his beloved Spiritual Father and Mother with the thought that they would all meet again in the celestial realms.

He journeyed quickly to his homeland, crossing several high and dangerous mountain passes to get there. When he arrived he found things just as he had seen in his dream. His mother had died, his house was in ruins, and the neighbours were afraid to go near it, thinking that evil ghosts inhabited it. His sister wandered homeless, none knew where. His field was choked with weeds.

He entered the ruin that was his house and found a mound with grass growing thickly over it. Moving the dirt he found the bones of what he knew to be his mother. He had the unbearable thought that he would never see his mother again and a deep sadness gripped his soul. He wept bitterly in his loneliness. Remembering his Guru's teachings on the transient nature of reality, he lay down using the mound as a pillow and entered into deep meditation. He soon passed over into the samadhi state in which he remained for seven days. On returning to normal consciousness, he reflected that the world now had nothing left to tempt him or bind him to it. He vowed again and again to himself that the life of solitary meditation was the only path for him.

Tubhaga Becomes Milarepa

Exchanging his house and land for some food, Tubhaga left his former homeland forever, and proceeded to the Draktar-Taso Cave, the first of many caves he was to inhabit over the remainder of his life.

He settled in the cave, not sleeping, but meditating continuously except for a single break once a day to prepare a meal of flour and water mixed with whatever root or edible plant he would find. At about this time Tubhaga gained proficiency in the yogic power of Tum-mo, the generation of the Ecstatic Internal Warmth, in which the body generates a great deal of heat. This allowed him to stay relatively warm through the cold Tibetan winters with nothing but a thin cotton covering, whereas most people had to wear thick wool and leather hides. For this reason he came to be called **Mila-repa** or 'Mila the cotton clad'.

Milarepa's daily routine of meditation continued for four years until his supply of flour ran out. This caused him great concern because he had vowed to himself not to return to the world for any reason – but with no food, he was afraid he might die

Milarepa, the yogi in a cave

without having attained liberation. He decided to walk about outside the cave in search of some kind of food.

Not far from the cave he found a sunny spot with springs of fresh water, an expansive view of the area, with a large quantity of nettles growing all about. He made a soup of nettle and found it to be somewhat palatable. This was now to become his sole source of food for some time to come. He continued his meditations on his new diet, but without any nurturing food, his body soon became emaciated and the hair on his body began to take on a greenish tinge from the nettles. He became very weak and often thought of opening the scroll that Marpa had given him for a time of dire need. But he continued to make progress in his meditations.

About this time some hunters chanced to be in the area after failing to find game. When they first laid eyes on Milarepa's pale green form, they fled in terror thinking he was not a man but some kind of evil spirit. But once assured that he was indeed a human like themselves, they lost their fear of him. They demanded that he share some of his provisions with them as they were out of food but Milarepa told them he had none to share. They did not believe him, so they searched the area and not finding anything, began to ill treat him. Three of them picked him up several times and dropped him causing him great pain, but in his misery he only pitied them and shed tears thinking of the evil karma they were creating for themselves. The fourth hunter entreated the others to stop ill-treating him and leave him alone as he did indeed seem to be a real lama for showing such forbearance over his ill-treatment. Before leaving, the fourth man requested Milarepa to remember him in his prayers since the man had done nothing to offend him, and then the group left, laughing boisterously. Later Milarepa learned that Divine retribution had overtaken them as they were arrested by the Governor of the province. The leader was killed and all but the fourth man, who had restrained the others from harming Milarepa, had their eyes pulled out.

The meditation continued and Milarepa grew even thinner. The hair on his body took on a more greenish colour. Again some hunters chanced upon his cave and also wanted provisions, but seeing that he was living only on nettles, they left him the remainder of their own provisions and a large quantity of meat. Milarepa was very grateful to have some real food and he began to take some daily. The food gave him a sense of bodily comfort and spiritual zeal, which he had not experienced in a long time and his meditations took on a new intensity. But eventually the food ran out and once again he fell back on his nettle broth for sustenance.

Several more years passed in this way and Milarepa's long lost sister Peta heard tales from hunters that had stumbled across his camp. They informed her that her brother was there and looked on the verge of death from starvation. She was amazed to hear that he was alive and decided to see him and find out if the rumours were true

Approaching the cave, Peta was horrified to see the emaciated green body of her brother, with protruding bones and sunken eyes. At first she took it to be some strange being or ghost but recognizing her brother's voice, she ran to him crying and bewailing their fate. She felt that they two were the most luckless people in the whole world. At this Milarepa explained that he was one of the most fortunate people in the world because he had attained to transcendent knowledge and Bodhi mind.

Peta had brought food and *chang*; and after partaking of some food Milarepa's mood was greatly elevated. However when he tried to meditate, he found that his mind was now disturbed and his body was experiencing various pains.

No matter how hard he tried to meditate he could no longer enter the samadhi state. Feeling there was no greater danger than not being able to continue with his meditations, he opened the scroll that Marpa had given him for just such a time of emergency. In the scroll he found the exact instructions needed for treating the present emergency and he immediately put the instructions into effect with the result that his meditations now increased as never before.

The knot of the central spinal column, along which the psychic energy flows, was now cleared at the plexus below the navel and the psychic energy current rose up his spine in its fullness. He now experienced a super sensuous calmness and clearness that far exceeded in its ecstatic intensity than any of the states he had previously reached.

He attained to new heights of realisation in which he saw that the highest state of Nirvana and the ordinary state of Samsaaric consciousness were opposite and inseparable states, resting on the base of the Ultimate Awareness. In his new realisation he could clearly see that the samsaric or phenomenal existence results when the Universal Mind is directed along the path of self centered and self oriented awareness, and that the Nirvanic state of transcendence results when it is directed on the path of selfless or altruistic awareness.

Greatly encouraged by this new development, Milarepa redoubled his zeal and began to develop the siddhis or yogic powers that accompany full enlightenment. His production of the inner vital heat also developed fully so that he could easily sit amongst the frozen snows and melt the ice into water. People started to talk about him, started to visit him so Milarepa decided to go to even more isolated caves.

As he was about to leave the area, his sister Peta came once again, bringing him some cloth for him to fasten into a garment for his naked body. She tried to dissuade him and suggested that he become a lama, so that he would get offerings in return for religious blessings. Milarepa refused, and taught her the doctrine of karma (i.e. the law of retribution) so that she would refrain from incurring any fresh debts from harmful actions.

While Peta was visiting, their aunt arrived, the aunt who had started the entire chain of events so many years back by seizing the property of Milarepa's widowed mother. The uncle who had conspired with her, had died, and she now deeply repented all she had done, and so she had brought a yak load of supplies and found Milarepa by asking about in the villages. Milarepa agreed to talk to her and delivered several religious discourses to her reminding her of all the sufferings and misery she had inflicted on them. In her state of misery, the aunt took his teachings to heart and went on her way, having been converted to a path that would confer eventual liberation. Peta also left, feeling somewhat at peace.

Milarepa now removed to Lapchi-Kang (Everest) and continued his meditation amidst the snows and isolation there. Altogether he meditated in twenty caves covering the region from Mount Kailas and Lapchi-Kang in Tibet to far off Nepal. It is said that besides his many human converts he also brought to enlightenment some superhuman (i.e. non-embodied) beings as well, including the Goddess Tseringma (one of the twelve guardian deities of Tibet who reside at Mt. Kailas). The Goddess came to tempt him with her powers during his meditations and instead was herself liberated.

During his travels over the 84 years of his life he met many worthy disciples that were destined to come under his tutelage. Highest among the disciples was Dvagpo Rimpoche (Gambopa). The most well known among them was Rechung who entreated him to tell in detail the story of his life. These two disciples were respectively like the sun and the moon.

Besides his two chief disciples, Milarepa had 25 additional highly accomplished disciples, both men and women, who became saints. Another hundred made such progress that they did not take rebirth. Another hundred and eight Great Ones obtained excellent experience and knowledge from meditation. A thousand sadhus and yogis, both men and women, renounced

Milarepa passes on

worldly life and lived lives of exemplary piety. Innumerable lay disciples formed a religious relationship with Milarepa so that the gateway to lower states of existence was closed to them forever.

A very rich and influential lama named Geshe Tsaphuwa heard of Mila's great fame and felt deeply jealous. Mila was invited to a feast, where he was seated as a guest of honour. All were bowing to him and Geshe had to do the same, though grudgingly. He tried testing Milarepa's knowledge, asking him to interpret a text.

"Having maintained pure awareness, I forgot the illusions of ignorance. Accustomed long to the meaning of wordless, I forgot how to play with phrases…as you are a master, you can explain it yourself," responded Milarepa.

Feeling further humiliated, Geshe decided to poison Milarepa. He mixed poison in yoghurt and sent it to Milarepa while he was having his meal.

Knowing that his time had come, Milarepa had the poisoned yoghurt. Then he sent word that all who had known him and had faith in him, and those who wished to meet him should come. A great number of people set out for his cave – where for many days Milarepa held discourses on the law of karma and the nature of reality.

Surrounded by his disciples, Milarepa entered a deep state of meditation. Thus he passed away at the age of 84. The sky and the whole environs of that place were full of lights and fragrance, and all who had gathered experienced a feeling of ecstasy.

A mandala was made, on which was erected a funeral cell. After the cremation, everyone saw the dakinis carry away a sphere of light into the sky, leaving nothing behind in the cremation cell.

Thus ended the life of Milarepa, whose line of teachings and practice, known as Kagyu (oral transmission lineage) is still alive and continues to spread all over the world.

PART VI

The Songs of Milarepa

The name by which Milarepa is known in Tibet is Jetsun Milarepa. 'Jetsun' is an honorific meaning 'holy', while 'Repa' means 'clad in cotton'. Mila was a family name. Hence, in English he may be called 'Holy Mila the Cotton-clad'.

The teachings of Milarepa are in the form of songs or poems, which talk about Dhamma, which is an important part of the Buddhist tradition. The closest in Pali literature to these songs are the utterances of Lord Buddha in the Sutta Nipaata, Udaana and Itivuttaka and also in the Dhammapada.

Milarepa's songs deal with renunciation and the dangers of Samsaara and impermanence. There are songs describing different aspects of Samsaara, such as birth, old age, sickness and death; relatives and wealth. Next are songs relating to practice – advice on how to practise and warnings about what not to do. Finally there are songs describing aspects of Milarepa's realisation – his contentment, happiness and non-attachment – and his blessings. Fortunately, Milarepa has also given an outline of his life in one of the songs.

Milarepa's teachings talk about the *impermanence* of all things, states, people, places, and that by not recognising this truth and by thinking in terms of permanence, self, etc., we come to experience unending *dissatisfaction*. Milarepa also points out the way to transcend this dissatisfaction and emphasises the keeping of precepts, concentrating the scattered mind and the development of wisdom. The 'Hundred Thousand Songs of Milarepa' mention the 'Whispered Transmission' of meditation instructions, which are imparted by the teacher to his disciples.

Buddha was well known for his remarkable ability in preaching exactly the right Dhamma to fit the situation and meet the understanding of those who listened. He did not teach the deep truths of Dhamma to those who were not prepared as yet to receive them and in a similar fashion, Milarepa also graded his teachings for varying circumstances and intelligences.

Like Lord Buddha, Milarepa taught Dhamma to all – to the emissary of a king and to shepherds, to nuns and wealthy ladies, to bhikkhus and yogis, to bandits and merchants. His conversion of the hunter, 'Chirawa Gwumbo Dorje', is as popular a story in Tibet, as is the pacifying of 'Angulimaal' by Lord Buddha in India.

At the age of 84, Jetsun Milarepa relinquished his body, passing away, surrounded by disciples, both human and celestial. For 900 years the traditions of meditation in which he trained his disciples have been handed down in Tibet. It has come to be known as the Ghagyupa or Kagyu (sometimes known as Kargyutpa), which is translated as the 'Whispered Transmission'.

In the time of Milarepa, as is evident from his songs; many bhikkhus spent long years in study but never gave much heed to practice. Scholar-bhikkhus of Tibet were, at that time, very able in arguing the finer points of Buddhist philosophy and well equipped with logic. But somehow, the urge to practise meditation was missing. This was true of the spiritual forebears of Milarepa (his immediate Guru, Marpa and of the Indian yogis, Naropa and Tilopa).

In several places Milarepa criticises those bhikkhus, and indeed anyone, who studies the Dhamma just for intellectual satisfaction or even for worldly advantage. Many sincere bhikkhus did approach him for meditation instructions and, thereafter, practised with him as their teacher. Milarepa was, therefore, a source for the spiritual regeneration of the Sangha in Tibet.

With his insistence upon the *practice* of Dhamma, Milarepa's life and teaching present striking similarities in many respects, to the Way as practised by the thudong (dhutanga) bhikkhu. The greatest difference is that a bhikkhu is bound to observe his Fundamental Precepts, which, as Milarepa did not have the bhikkhu ordination, he did not have to keep. Nevertheless, even a quick look at his life after he began his practice would reveal that he scrupulously maintained those injunctions given to him by his teacher, Marpa, as well as cultivating the twin bases of moral conduct in the Dhamma, Wisdom and Compassion.

Though he had not the formal ordination of a bhikkhu and wore not the monks' robes, yet Milarepa, according to definitions given in the Dhammapada, was indeed a true bhikkhu.

"He who has no attachment whatsoever towards the 'mind-and-body' and who does not grieve for what he has not, – he indeed, is called a bhikkku. Whoso herein, has abandoned both merit and demerit, he who is holy, he who walks with understanding in this world, – he indeed, is called a bhikkhu."

One day, after leaving his cave to collect firewood,
Milarepa returned to find five Indian demons with eyes as
large as saucers, who he thought to be apparitions of the
deities who disliked him. As he had never given them any
offering, he then began to sing:

Complimentary Song to the Deities of
Red Rock Jewel Valley

This lonely spot where stands my hut,
Is a place pleasing to the Buddhas,
A place where accomplished beings dwell,
A refuge where I dwell alone.

Above Red Rock Jewel Valley,
White clouds are gliding;
Below, the Tsang River gently flows;
Wild vultures wheel between.

Bees are humming among the flowers,
Intoxicated by their fragrance;
In the trees, birds swoop and dart,
Filling the air with their song.

In Red Rock Jewel Valley,

Young sparrows learn to fly,
Monkeys love to leap and swing,
And beasts to run and race,
While I practise the Two Bodhi-minds and love to meditate.

Ye local demons, ghosts and gods,
All friends of Milarepa,
Drink the nectar of kindness and compassion,
Then return to your abodes.

*

*One day, Milarepa's patrons from Dro Tang came to visit
him. They asked him what benefits Junpan Nanka Tsang
had to offer. In reply, Milarepa sang:*

I pray to my Guru, the Holy One.
Listen, my patrons, and I will tell you,
The merits of this place.

In the goodly quiet of this Sky Castle of Junpan,
High above, dark clouds gather;
Deep blue and far below flows the River Tsang.

At my back the Red Rock of Heaven rises;
At my feet, wild flowers bloom, vibrant and profuse;
At my cave's edge (wild) beasts roam, roar and grunt;
In the sky vultures and eagles circle freely,
While from heaven drifts the drizzling rain.
Bees hum and buzz with their chanting;
Mares and foals gambol and gallop wildly;
The brook chatters past pebbles and rocks;
Through the trees monkeys leap and swing;
And larks carol in sweet song.

The timely sounds I hear are all my fellows.
The merits of this place are inconceivable –
I now relate them to you in this song.

Oh good patrons,
Pray follow my Path and my example;
Abandon evil, and practise good deeds.
Spontaneously from my heart,
I give you this instruction.

★

One day, some villagers from Ragma came to see Milarepa.
They asked him, "Why do you like this place so much?
Why is it that you are so happy here? Pray, tell us what you
think of all these things?" In answer,
Milarepa sang:

Here is the Bodhi-Place, quiet and peaceful.
The snow-mountain, the dwelling-place of deities,
Stands high above;
Below, far from here in the village, my faithful patrons live;
Surrounding it are mountains nestling in white snow.
In the foreground stand the wish-granting trees;
In the valley lie vast meadows, blooming wild.
Around the pleasant, sweet-scented lotus, insects hum;
Along the banks of the stream,
And in the middle of the lake,
Cranes bend their necks, enjoying the scene,
And are content.

On the branches of the trees, the wild birds sing;
When the wind blows gently, slowly dances the weeping
willow;
On the treetops monkeys bound and leap in joy;
In the wild green pastures graze the scattered herds,
And merry shepherds, gay and free from worry,

Sing cheerful songs and play upon their reeds.
The people of the world, with burning desires and craving,
Distracted by affairs, become the slaves of earth.

From the top of the Resplendent Gem Rock,
I, the yogi, see these things.
Observing them, I know that they are fleeting and transient;
Contemplating them, I realise that comforts and pleasure,
Are merely mirages and water-reflections.

I see this life as a conjuration and a dream.
Great compassion rises in my heart,
For those without a knowledge of this truth.
The food I eat is the Space-Void;
My meditation is Dhyaana – beyond distraction.

Myriad visions and various feelings all appear before me –
Strange indeed are Samsaric phenomena!
Truly amazing are the dharmas in the Three Worlds,
Oh, what a wonder, what a marvel!
Void is their nature, yet everything is manifested.

✷

This song was sung to a young, well-dressed girl who after asking Milarepa about his father and mother, brothers and sisters, further enquired: "But do you also have any Samsaaric companions, sons and belongings?" Milarepa then sang in reply:

At first, my experiences in Samsaara,
Seemed most pleasant and delightful;
Later, I learned about its lessons;
In the end, I found a Devil's Prison.
These are my thoughts and feelings on Samsaara.
So I made up my mind to renounce it.

At first, one's friend is like a smiling angel;
Later, she turns into a fierce exasperated woman;
But in the end a demoness is she.
These are my thoughts and feelings on companions.
So I made up my mind to renounce a friend.

At first, the sweet boy smiles, a Babe of Heaven;
Later, he makes trouble with the neighbours;
In the end, he is my creditor and foe.
These are my thoughts and feelings about children.
So I renounced both sons and nephews.

At first, money is like the Wish-fulfilling Gem;
Later, one cannot do without it;
In the end, one feels a penniless beggar.
These are my thoughts and feelings about money.
So I renounced both wealth and goods.

When I think of these experiences,
I cannot help but practise Dharma;
When I think of Dharma,
I cannot help but offer it to others.
When death approaches,
I shall then have no regret.

*

On his way to Shri Ri to meditate, Milarepa lodged at an inn where a merchant, Dhawa Norbu, was also staying with a large retinue. Milarepa begged alms from him upon which the merchant remarked that it would be better for him to work to support himself. Milarepa pointed out that enjoying pleasures now is the source for more suffering in the future. Then he said: "Now listen to my song."

The Eight Reminders

Castles and crowded cities are the places,
Where now you love to stay;
But remember that they will fall to ruins,
After you have departed from this earth!
Pride and vain glory are the lure,
Which now you love to follow;
But remember, when you are about to die,
They offer you no shelter and no refuge!

Kinsmen and relatives are the people now,
With whom you love to live;
But remember that you must leave them all behind,
When from this world you pass away!
Servants, wealth and children,
Are things you love to hold;
But remember, at the time of your death,

Your empty hands can take nothing with you!

Vigour and health,
Are dearest to you now;
But remember, at the moment of your death,
Your corpse will be bundled up and borne away!

Now your organs are clear,
Your flesh and blood are strong and vigorous;
But remember, at the moment of your death,
They will no longer be at your disposal!
Sweet and delicious foods are things,
That now you love to eat;
But remember, at the moment of your death,
Your mouth will let the spittle flow!

When of all this I think,
I cannot help but seek the Buddha's Teachings!
The enjoyments and the pleasures of this world,
For me have no attraction.

I, Milarepa, sing of the Eight Reminders,
At the Guest House in Garakhache of Tsang.
With these clear words I give this helpful warning;
I urge you to observe and practise them!

★

Milarepa once said to Shindormo, his patroness: "But if you have a precious human body and have been born at a time and place in which the Buddhist religion prevails, it is very foolish indeed not to practise the Dharma." Milarepa thus sang:

At the feet of the Translator Marpa, I prostrate myself,
And sing to you, my faithful patrons.

How stupid it is to sin with recklessness,
While the pure Dharma spreads all about you.
How foolish to spend your lifetime without meaning,
When a precious human body is so rare a gift.

How ridiculous to cling to prison-like cities,
And remain there.
How laughable to fight and quarrel,
With your wives and relatives,
Who do but visit you.
How senseless to cherish sweet and tender words,
Which are but empty echoes in a dream.
How silly to disregard one's life by fighting foes,
Who are but frail flowers.

How foolish it is when dying,
To torment oneself with thoughts of family,

Which bind one to Maya's mansion.
How stupid to stint on property and money,
Which are a debt on loan from others.
How ridiculous it is to beautify and deck the body,
Which is a vessel full of filth.
How silly to strain each nerve for wealth and goods,
And neglect the nectar of the inner teachings!

In a crowd of fools, the clear and sensible
Should practise the Dharma, as do I.

★

A yogi who had great faith in Milarepa came with other patrons, bringing copious offerings, and they asked Milarepa, how he had managed to undergo the trials of his probationship and had exerted himself... Milarepa answered with...

The Six Resolutions

When one has lost interest in this world,
His faith and longing for the Dharma is confirmed.

To relinquish one's home ties is very hard;
Only by leaving one's native land,
Can one be immune from anger.

It is hard to conquer burning passions,
Towards relatives and close friends;
The best way to quench them,
Is to break all associations.

One never feels that one is rich enough;
Contented, he should wear humble cotton clothes.
He may thus conquer much desire and craving.

It is hard to avoid worldly attractions;

By adhering to humbleness,
Longing for vain glory is subdued.

It is hard to conquer pride and egotism;
So, like the animals,
Live in the mountains.

My dear and faithful patrons!
Such is the real understanding,
That stems from perseverance.
I wish you all to practise deeds that are meaningful,
And amass all merits!

★

*Milarepa went out one day for alms and coming to a
meeting of Dharma-followers, was ridiculed. One of them,
however, recognized him and said: "To inspire those
attending this meeting, therefore, please now sing for us."
In response, Milarepa sang a song.*

The Ocean of Samsaara

Alas, is not Samsaara like the sea?
Drawing as much water as one pleases,
It remains the same without abating.
Are not the Three Precious Ones like Mount Sumeru,
That never can be shaken by anyone?

Are there Mongol bandits invading yogis' cells?
Why, then, do great yogis stay in towns and villages?
Are not people craving for rebirth and *bardo?
Why, then, do they cling so much to their disciples?
Are woollen clothes in the next life more expensive?
Why, then, do women make so much of them here?
Do people fear that Sa.msaara may be emptied?
Why, then, do priests and laymen hanker after children?
Are you reserving food and drink for your next life?
Why, then, do men and women not give to charity?
Is there any misery in Heaven above?

Why, then, do so few plan to go there?
Is there any joy below in Hell?
Why, then, do so many prepare to visit there?
Do you not know that all sufferings,
And Lower Realms are the result of sins?
Surely you know that if you now practise virtue,
When death comes you will have peace of mind,
And no regrets.

* The realm of the afterlife is called the world of bardo, the interval between death and the next rebirth.

★

Upon the arrival of autumn, Milarepa decided to leave
Upper Lowo where he had been preaching the Dharma
during the summer, and go to Di Se Snow Mountain. His
patrons gave him a farewell party, circling round him, and
made him offerings and obeisance. They said: "Be kind
enough to give us, your disciples, some instructions and
advice." Milarepa then emphasised the transiency of all
beings, admonishing them to practise Dharma earnestly.
And he sang...

The Song of Transience with Eight Similes

Faithful disciples here assembled (ask yourselves):
"Have I practised Dharma with great earnestness?
Has the deepest faith arisen in my heart?"
He who wants to practise Dharma and gain,
Non-regressive faith,
Should listen to this exposition of the Mundane Truths,
And ponder well their meaning.
Listen to these parables and metaphors:

A painting in gold,
Flowers of turquoise blue,
Floods in the vale above,
Rice in the vale below,

Abundance of silk,
A jewel of value,
The crescent moon,
And a precious son –
These are the eight similes.

No one has sung before,
Such casual words (on this),
No one can understand their meaning,
If he heeds not the whole song.

The gold painting fades when it is completed –
This shows the illusory nature of all beings,
This proves the transient nature of all things.
Think, *then* you will practise Dharma.

The lovely flowers of turquoise blue,
Are destroyed in time by frost –
This shows the illusory nature of all beings,
This proves the transient nature of all things.
Think!, *then* you will practise Dharma.
The flood sweeps strongly down the vale above,
Soon becoming weak and tame in the plain below –
This shows the illusory nature of all beings,
This proves the transient nature of all things.
Think, *then* you will practise Dharma.

Rice grows in the vale below;
Soon with a sickle it is reaped,
This shows the illusory nature of all beings,
This proves the transient nature of all things.
Think!, *then* you will practise Dharma.

Elegant silken cloth,
Soon with a knife is cut –
This shows the illusory nature of all beings,
This proves the transient nature of all things.
Think!, *then* you will practise Dharma.

The precious jewel that you cherish,
Soon will belong to others –
This shows the illusory nature of all beings,
This proves the transient nature of all things.
Think!, *then* you will practise Dharma.

The pale moonbeams soon will fade and vanish –
This shows the illusory nature of all beings,
This proves the transient nature of all things.
Think!, *then* you will practise Dharma.

A precious son is born;
Soon he is lost and gone –
This shows the illusory nature of all beings,

This proves the transient nature of all things.
Think!, *then* you will practise Dharma.
These are the eight similes I sing.
I hope you will remember and practise them.

Affairs and business will drag on forever,
So lay them down and practise now the Dharma.
If you think tomorrow is the time to practise,
Suddenly you find that life has slipped away.
Who can tell when death will come?

Ever think of this,
And devote yourselves to Dharma practice.

★

Travelling with his disciples, Milarepa came to Din Ri Namar where he enquired for the name of its outstanding patron. Learning that the physician Yang Nge was a devoted Buddhist, he proceeded to his house, where the physician said, "It is said that Milarepa can use anything at hand as a metaphor for preaching. Now please use the bubbles of water in this ditch before us as a metaphor and give us a discourse." In response, Milarepa sang a song...

The Fleeting Bubbles

I pay homage to my gracious Guru –
Pray make everyone here think of the Dharma!
As he said once, "Like bubbles is,
This life, transient and fleeting –
In it no assurance can be found."
A layman's life is like a thief,
Who sneaks into an empty house.
Know you not the folly of it?

Youth is like a summer flower –
Suddenly it fades away.
Old age is like a fire spreading,
Through the fields – suddenly 'tis at your heels.
The Buddha once said, "Birth and death,

Are like sunrise and sunset –
Now come, now go."
Sickness is like a little bird,
Wounded by a sling.
Know you not, health and strength,
Will in time desert you?
Death is like an oil-dry lamp,
(After its last flicker).
Nothing, I assure you,
In this world is permanent.
Evil Karma is like a waterfall,
Which I have never seen flow upward.
A sinful man is like a poisonous tree –
If you lean on it, you will injured be.
Transgressors are like frost-bitten peas –
Like spoiled fat, they ruin everything.
Dharma-practisers are like peasants in the field –
With caution and vigour they will be successful.
The Guru is like medicine and nectar –
Relying on him, one will win success.
Discipline is like a watchman's tower –
Observing it, one will attain Accomplishment.
The Law of Karma is like Samsaara's wheel –
Whoever breaks it will suffer a great loss.
Samsaara is like a poisonous thorn,
In the flesh – if not pulled out,

The poison will increase and spread.
The coming of death is like the shadow,
Of a tree at sunset –
It runs fast and none can halt it.
When that time comes,
What else can help but Holy Dharma?
Though Dharma is the fount of victory.
Those who aspire to it are rare.
Scores of men are tangled in,
The miseries of Samsaara;
Into this misfortune born,
They strive by plunder and theft for gain.

He who talks on Dharma,
With elation is inspired,
But when a task is set him,
He is wrecked and lost.
Dear patrons, do not talk too much,
But practise the Holy Dharma.

★

"This is indeed very helpful to my mind," commented the physician, "but please preach still further for me on the truth of Karma and the suffering of birth, old age, illness and death, thus enabling me to gain a deeper conviction in Buddhadharma." In response, Milarepa sang:

Please listen to these words,
Dear friends here assembled.

When you are young and vigorous,
You ne'er think of old age coming,
But it approaches slow and sure,
Like a seed growing underground.

When you are strong and healthy,
You ne'er think of sickness coming,
But it descends with sudden force,
Like a stroke of lightning.

When involved in worldly things,
You ne'er think of death's approach,
Quick it comes like thunder,
Crashing 'round your head.

Sickness, old age and death,

Ever meet each other,
As do hands and mouth.
Waiting for his prey in ambush,
Yama is ready for his victim,
When disaster catches him.
Sparrows fly in single file. Like them,
Life, death and bardo follow one another.
Never apart from you,
Are these three 'visitors'.
Thus thinking, fear you not,
Your sinful deeds?

Like strong arrows in ambush waiting,
Rebirth in Hell, as Hungry Ghost, or Beast,
Is (the destiny) waiting to catch you.
If once into their traps you fall,
Hard will you find it to escape.

Do you not fear the miseries,
You experienced in the past?
Surely you will feel much pain,
If misfortunes attack you?
The woes of life succeed one another,
Like the sea's incessant waves,
One has barely passed, before,
The next one takes its place.

Until you are liberated, pain,
And pleasure come and go at random,
Like passers-by encountered in the street.

Pleasures are precarious,
Like bathing in the sun;
Transient, too, as snowstorms,
Which come without warning.
Remembering these things,
Why not practise the Dharma?

★

*Rechungpa, after returning from India, had contracted
the disease of pride and in various ways Milarepa tried to
cure him. As his disciple required food, they went for alms
but were abused by an old woman who declared that she
had no food. The next morning they found her dead and
Milarepa said: "Rechungpa, like this woman, every sentient
being is destined to die, but seldom do people think of
this fact. So they lose many opportunities to practise the
Dharma. Both you and I should remember this incident
and learn a lesson from it." Whereupon, he sang:*

The Song of Transiency and Delusion

When the transience of life strikes deeply into one's heart,
One's thoughts and deeds will naturally accord with Dharma.
If repeatedly and continuously one thinks about death,
One can easily conquer the demons of laziness.
No one knows when death will descend upon him –
Just as this woman last night!
Rechungpa, do not be harsh, and listen to your Guru!
Behold, all manifestations in the outer world,
Are ephemeral like a dream last night!
One feels utterly lost in sadness,
When one thinks of this passing dream.
Rechungpa, have you completely wakened,

From this great puzzlement?
Oh, the more I think of this,
The more I aspire to Buddha and the Dharma.

The pleasure-yearning human body is an ungrateful creditor.
Whatever good you do to it,
It always plants the seeds of pain.

This human body is a bag of filth and dirt;
Never be proud of it, Rechungpa,
But listen to my song!

When I look back at my body,
I see it as a mirage-city;
Though I may sustain it for a while,
It is doomed to extinction.
When I think of this,
My heart is filled with grief!
Rechungpa, would you not cut off Samsaara?
Oh, the more I think of this,
The more I think of Buddha and the Dharma!

A vicious person can never attain happiness.
Errant thoughts are the cause of all regrets,
Bad dispositions are the cause of all miseries,
Never be voracious, oh Rechungpa,

But listen to my song!
When I look back at my clinging mind,
It appears like a short-lived sparrow in the woods –
Homeless, and with nowhere to sleep;
When I think of this, my heart is filled with grief.
Rechungpa, will you let yourself indulge in ill-will?
Oh, the more I think of this,
The more I aspire to Buddha and the Dharma!

Human life is as precarious,
As a single slim hair of a horse's tail,
Hanging on the verge of breaking;
It may be snuffed out at anytime,
Like this old woman was last night!
Do not cling to this life, Rechungpa,
But listen to my song!

When I observe inwardly my breathings,
I see they are transient, like the fog;
They may vanish any moment into nought.
When I think of this, my heart is filled with grief.
Rechungpa, do you not want to conquer,
That insecurity now?
Oh, the more I think of this,
The more I aspire to Buddha and the Dharma.

To be close to wicked kinsmen only causes hatred.
The case of this old woman is a very good lesson.
Rechungpa, stop your wishful-thinking,
And listen to my song!
When I look at friends and consorts,
They appear as passers-by in the bazaar;
Meeting with them is only temporary,
But separation is forever!
When I think of this, my heart is filled with grief.
Rechungpa, do you not want to cast aside,
All worldly associations?
Oh, the more I think of this,
The more I think of Buddha and the Dharma.

A rich man seldom enjoys,
The wealth that he has earned;
This is the mockery of Karma and Samsaara,
Money and jewels gained through stinginess and toil,
Are like this old woman's bag of food.
Do not be covetous, Rechungpa,
But listen to my song!

When I look at the fortunes of the rich,
They appear to me like honey to the bees –
Hard work, serving only for others' enjoyment,
Is the fruit of their labour.

When I think of this, my heart is filled with grief.
Rechungpa, do you not want to open,
The treasury within your mind?
Oh, the more I think of this,
The more I aspire to Buddha and His Teachings.

★

When Milarepa was sitting in meditation, a frightened deer dashed by, followed by a hound. By the power of his loving-kindness and compassion, Milarepa made them lie down, one on either side of him, and then preached to them. Then came the fierce and proud hunter, Chirawa Gwunbo Dorje, who was enraged by the sight of Milarepa and shot an arrow at him, but missed. Milarepa sang to him and his heart began to turn to the Dharma. Then the hunter saw that Milarepa was living an austere life and great faith arose in him. He wished then to practise Dharma after talking with his family but Milarepa warned him that his present meritorious thought might change, and he sang:

Hearken, hearken, huntsman!
Though the thunder crashes,
It is but empty sound;
Though the rainbow is richly-coloured,
It will soon fade away.
The pleasures of this world are like dream-visions;
Though one enjoys them, they are the source of sin.
Though all we see may seem to be eternal,
It will soon fall to pieces and will disappear.

Yesterday perhaps one had enough or more,

All today is gone and nothing's left;
Last year one was alive, this year one dies.
Good food turns into poison,
And the beloved companion turns into a foe.
Harsh words and complaints requite,
Good-will and gratitude.
Your sins hurt no one but yourself.
Among one hundred heads, you value most your own.
In all ten fingers, if one is cut, you feel the pain.
Among all things you value, yourself is valued most.
The time has come for you to help yourself.

Life flees fast. Soon death,
Will knock upon your door.
It is foolish, therefore, one's devotion to postpone.
What else can loving kinsmen do,
But throw one into Samsaara?
To strive for happiness hereafter,
Is more important than to seek it now.
The time has come for you to rely upon a Guru,
The time has come to practise Dharma.

★

Milarepa: "If one is really determined to free oneself from
the sufferings of Samsaara, such as birth, old age, illness,
death, and so on, he will have peace of mind all the time
and will not need to make any effort. Otherwise, he
should bear in mind that the sufferings in a future life could
be much more durable and longer-lasting than those in
this life, and the burden could also be much heavier. It
is, therefore, of paramount importance to take steps to
prepare for the next life." This was said to some young
men from his native country, who asked how they could
extricate themselves from worldly affairs.
Then, Milarepa said: "I will sing a song for you."

We sentient beings moving in the world,
Float down the flowing stream,
Of the Four Sufferings.
Compared to this, how much more formidable,
Are the unceasing future lives in Samsaara,
Why not, then, prepare a boat for the "crossing"?

The state of our future lives is far more fearful,
And deserving of far more concern,
Than are the dreadful demons, ghosts and Yama,
So why not prepare for yourself a guide?

Even the dread passions – craving, hatred and blindness –
Are not so fearful,
As the state of our (unknown) future,
So why not prepare for yourself an antidote?

Great is the Kingdom of the Three Realms of Samsaara,
But greater is the endless road of birth-and-death,
So why not prepare for yourself provisions?
It will be better if you practise Dharma,
If you have no assurance in yourselves.

*Milarepa said: "A human body, free and opportune, is
as precious as a jewel, and to have a chance to practise
the Dharma is likewise very rare. Also, to find one
serious Buddhist in a hundred is difficult! Considering the
difficulties of meeting the right Gurus, and other necessary
favourable conditions for practising Buddhism, you should
deem yourselves very fortunate that you have now met all
these requirements. Do not, therefore, waste them, but
practise the Dharma."*

*

Shiwa Aui, a leading disciple of Milarepa, once asked his
Master, when the latter was nearing the end of his life:
"Please tell us what are the joys and miseries that sentient
beings experience in the Six Realms? Especially, please tell
us what are the pleasures devas enjoy?" Milarepa replied:
"Do not be fascinated by the pleasures of heavenly beings;
they also have miseries – like this..."

The pleasures enjoyed by men and devas,
Are like the amusements of the Heavenly Yak:
It may low like thunder,
But what good can it do?

(Swooning in a state of trance),
The devas in the four Formless Heavens,
Cannot distinguish good from evil.
Because their minds are dull and callous,
Insensible, they have no feeling.
In unconscious stupefaction,
They live many kalpas in a second.
What a pity that they know it not!
Alas, these heavenly births,
Have neither sense nor value.
When they think vicious thoughts,
They start to fall again.

As to the reason for their fall,
(Scholars), with empty words,
Have dried their mouths in explanations.

In the Heavens of Form,
The devas of the five higher and twelve lower realms,
Can only live until their merits are exhausted.
Their virtues are essentially conditional,
And their Karma basically Samsaaric.

Those Dharma-practisers subject to worldly desires,
And those 'great yogis' wrapped in stillness,
Have yet to purify their minds;
Huge may be their claims and boasts,
But habitual thought-seeds,
In their minds are deeply rooted.
After a long dormant time,
Evil thoughts again will rise.
When their merits and fortunes are consumed;
They to the Lower Realms will go once more!

If I explain the horror of a deva's death,
You will be disheartened and perplexed.
Bear this in your mind and ever meditate!

★

In a sad mood, the disciples then asked Milarepa to preach
to them of the sufferings of the asuras.
In response, he sang:

Great are asuras' sufferings.
Misled by malignant thoughts,
To all they bring misfortunes,
Knowing not their true Self-mind,
Their deeds are self-deceiving,
Their feelings coarse, their senses crude,
Deeming all to be their foes,
Not even for a moment,
Can they know the truth.
Evil by nature, they can hardly bear a loss;
Harder is benevolence for them to cherish.
Blinded by the Karma-of-Belligerence,
Never can they take good counsel.

All nature such as this is caused,
By seeking pleasures for oneself,
And bearing harmful thoughts towards others.
Pride, favouritism, vanity and hatred,
Are the evil Karmic forces,
That drag one to a lower birth,
Making sinful deeds more easy.

Ripening Karma brings (to them),
An instinctive hatred;
Failing to distinguish right from wrong,
They can hardly be helped by any means.
Bear, oh my disciples, this in your minds,
And meditate with perseverance all your lives!

★

Shiwa Aui said, "Now please tell us about the sufferings of human beings." In answer, Milarepa sang:

We human beings are endowed with power,
To do good, or evil deeds;
This is because our body (personality),
Is made of all Six Elements.

You junior Repas who desire to be great scholars,
Should know the 'Kernel and shell' of Buddhism.
Lest learning lead you only to confusion.

Knowing not the *root of mind*,
Useless is it to meditate for years.
Without sincerity and willingness,
Rich offerings have no real meaning.

Without giving impartial aid to all,
Patronage of one's favourite is wrong.
Knowing not the right counsel for each man,
Blunt talk will only bring trouble and discord.

He who knows the appropriate way,
To help men of diverse dispositions,
Can use expedient words for kind and fruitful purposes.

He who knows but little of himself,
Can harm many by his ignorance.
When good-will arises in one's mind,
Stones, trees and earth all become seeds of virtue.
Again, an over-punctilious person,
Knows not how to relax;
A gluttonous dog knows not what is hunger;
A brazen Guru knows not what is fear.

Rich men are wretched creatures with their money,
Poor men are wretched creatures without money.
Alas, with, or without money, both are miserable!
Happiness will come, dear children,
If you can practise the Dharma.
Remember then, my words, and practise with perseverance.

★

"It is very true that human beings suffer like this," agreed the disciples. "Now please tell us about the sufferings in the three miserable realms, even though, just to mention them may be distressing. Also, to spur our spiritual efforts, please preach to us of the causes of Hell and its woe."
In response, Milarepa sang:

Those who, for meat and blood,
Slaughter living beings,
Will in the Eight Hot Hells be burned.
But if they can remember the Good Teachings,
Soon will they be emancipated.
Ruthless robbers who strike and kill,
Wrongly eating others' food,
While clinging to their own with greed,
Will fall into the Eight Cold Hells.
Yet if they do not hold wrong views against the Dharma,
It is said that their time for deliverance will come.
(The Holy Scriptures) also say,
Whene'er the denizens of hell,
Recall the name of Buddha,
Delivered will they be immediately.

Ever repeating sinful deeds means,
Dominance by vice and evil Karma.

Fiends filled with the craving for pleasures,
Murder even their parents and Gurus,
Rob the Three Gems of their treasure,
Revile and accuse falsely the Precious Ones,
And condemn the Dharma as untrue;
In the Hell-of-unceasing-torment,
These evil doers will be burned;
Far from them alas, is Liberation.
This, my sons, will certainly distress you,
So into Dharma throw your hearts,
And devote yourselves to meditation!

★

"For the benefit of sentient beings, please tell us now about
the sufferings of the Hungry Ghosts." In reply,
Milarepa sang:

Hungry Ghosts, seeing all forms as foes,
Run from each successive terror.
Wild beasts fight and eat each other.
Who of them is to blame?
The sufferings of the Hungry Ghosts,
Grow from their stinginess.
Like a rat is he who fails,
To give alms when he is rich,
Begrudges food when he has plenty,
Gives no food to others, but checks,
Them over, counts and stores them –
Discontented day and night.
At the time of death he sees,
That his hard-earned wealth,
Will be enjoyed by others.

Caught in bardo by the agony of loss,
As a Hungry Ghost he lives his life.
Due to his delusive thoughts,
He suffers thirst and hunger.
When he sees his goods enjoyed by others,

He is tormented by avarice and hate.
Again and again will he thus fall down (to Hell).
I, the great Yogi of Strength,
Now sing for you the woes,
Of Hungry Ghosts. Dear sons,
And disciples here assembled, think on,
My words and meditate with perseverance!

★

*Shiwa Aui then requested, "Now please tell us of the
sufferings of animals." Whereupon Milarepa sang:*

Animals, alas, are ignorant and benighted;
Most stupid men will incarnate amongst them.
Blind and enslaved by evil Karma,
The ignorant know not Dharma's Truth.
Blind both to evil and to virtue,
They quickly waste their lives away.
Unable to reason and use symbols,
They act like blind automations;
Unable to distinguish wrong from right,
Like maniacs, they do much wrong.
Some people even say 'tis good,
(To be an animal);
Since it does neither regret nor repent,
Alas! How foolish is this thought!
Then, all stupid life-takers,
Will incarnate as beasts;
The fools who know not right from wrong,
And those who harbour vicious thoughts,
Will incarnate as common brutes.
Hard it is for me to describe,
Their Karmas, but think on my words,
And cultivate your minds.

*

Milarepa once took Rechungpa to the market of Nya Non in order to further his spirit of renunciation. Many butchers had gathered there. The meat was piled up like walls, animals' heads were stacked in huge heaps, skins were scattered over the ground, and blood ran like water in a pond. In addition, rows of livestock were fastened to the stakes for slaughtering.... Whereupon with overwhelming compassion, Milarepa sang:

How pitiful are sentient beings in Samsaara!
Looking upward to the Path of Liberation,
How can one feel aught but sorrow for these sinful men.
How foolish and sad it is to indulge in killing,
When by good luck and Karma one has a human form.
How sad it is to do an act,
That in the end will hurt oneself.
How sad it is to build a sinful wall,
Of meat made of one's dying parents' flesh?
How sad it is to see,
Meat eaten and blood flowing.
How sad it is to know confusions,
And delusions fill the minds of men.

How sad it is to find but vice,
Not love, in peoples' hearts.

How sad it is to see,
That Blindness veils all men,
Who cherish sinful deeds.

Craving causes misery,
While worldly deeds bring pain.
With this in mind one feels sorrowful,
Thinking thus, one searches for a cure.
When I think of those who never,
Take heed for their future lives,
But indulge in evil deeds,
I feel most disturbed and sad,
And deeply fearful for them.
Rechungpa, seeing all these things,
Don't you remember Holy Dharma?
Don't you in Samsaara lose all heart?
Rouse the spirit of renunciation,
Go, Rechungpa, to the cave to meditate!

Heed the bounty of your Guru,
And avoid all sinful deeds,
Casting worldly things aside,
Stay firm in your practice,
Keep your good vows,
And devote your life to meditation.

★

A very beautiful girl of about fifteen years of age, whose name was Bardarbom said to Milarepa: "By merely meeting you I shall have accumulated a great deal of merit," and begged to be taken as his servant and disciple. Milarepa replied, "If you seriously want to practise the Dhamma, you must learn that worldly affairs are your enemies and renounce them." And he sang a song called:

The Four Renunciations

Listen, you fortunate girl,
You who have wealth and faith!

Future lives last longer than this life –
Do you know how to make provision?
Giving with niggardly heart,
As if feeding a strange watch-dog,
Only brings more harm than good –
Bringing nothing in return but a vicious bite,
Renounce parsimony, now that you know its evil.

Listen, you fortunate girl!
We know less of this life than the next one.
Have you prepared and lit your lamp?
Should it not be ready,
Meditate on the "Great Light".
If you choose to help an ungrateful foe,

You will gain not a friend, but damage.
Beware of acting blindly:
Beware of this evil and discard it.

Listen, you fortunate girl.
Future lives are worse than this life –
Have you a guide or escort for your journey?
If you have not the right companion,
Rely on the holy Dharma.
Beware of relatives and kinsmen;
They hinder and oppose (the Dharma).
They never help but only harm one.
Did you know that your kinsmen are your foes?
If this be true, surely you should leave them.

Listen, you fortunate girl.
The journey in the future life,
Is more hazardous than this one –
Have you prepared a fine horse of perseverance for it?
If not, you should strive hard and work with diligence.
The excitement of the start will soon diminish;
Beware the foe, "Inertness" , which makes one go astray.
Of no avail are hurry and excitement, which only harm one.
Do you yet know that your enemies are laziness and caprice?
If you understand my words,
You should cast them both away.

★

Going to Bardarbom's house for alms, Milarepa
encountered "an ugly old woman with a handful of ashes".
She rushed at him, shouting, "You miserable yogi-beggars!
I never see you in one place! In the summer you all show
up begging for milk and butter! In the winter you all come
for grain! I'll wager you wanted to sneak in to steal my
daughter's and daughter-in-law's jewellery!" Grumbling
and trembling with rage, she was about to throw the ashes
at Milarepa, when he said, "Wait a minute, grandmother!
Please listen to me!" He then sang...

A Song with Nine Meanings

Above is the auspicious Heaven,
Below are the Three Paths of Misery,
In between, are those who are not free,
To choose their birth.

These three all converge on you.
Grandmother, you are an angry woman,
And dislike the Dharma!
Qusestion your own thoughts and your mind examine.
You should practise the Buddha's Teaching,
You need a qualified and dependable Guru,
Think carefully, dear lady;

When you were first sent here,
Did you dream that you would become an old nanny-goat?

In the morning you get up from bed,
In the evening you go to sleep,
In between, you do the endless housework;
You are engrossed in these three things.
Grandmother, you are an unpaid maid.
Qusestion your own thoughts and your mind examine.
You should practise the Buddha's Teaching,
You need a qualified and dependable Guru,
And then things may be different for you.

The head of the family is the most important one,
Income and earnings are the next most longed-for things,
Then sons and nephews are wanted most.
By these three you are bound,
Grandmother, for yourself you have no share.
Question your own thoughts and your mind examine.
You should practise the Buddha's Teaching,
You need a qualified and dependable Guru,
And then things may be different for you.

Attaining what you want even though you steal,
Getting what you desire even though you rob,
Fighting your foe without regard to death and wounds,

To these three things you are subjected.

Grandmother, you are burned up with fury,
When you come upon your foe.
Question your own thoughts and your mind examine.
You should practise the Buddha's Teaching,
You need a qualified and dependable Guru,
And then things may be different for you.

Gossip about other women and their manners,
Is what interests you;
To the affairs of your own son and nephew,
You pay attention,
To talk of widows and relatives is your delight.
These three things enchant you.
Grandmother, are you so gentle when you gossip?
Question your own thoughts and your mind examine.
You should practise the Buddha's Teaching,
You need a qualified and dependable Guru,
And then things may be different for you.

To lift you from a chair is like pulling out a peg;
With feeble legs you waddle like a thieving goose;
Earth and stone seem to shatter when you drop into a seat;
Senile and clumsy is your body,
Grandmother, you have no choice but to obey.

Question your own thoughts and your mind examine.
You should practise the Buddha's Teaching,
What you require is a qualified and dependable Guru,
And from that you may find out how you have changed.
Your skin is creased with wrinkles;
Your bones stand out sharply from your shrunken flesh,
You are deaf, dumb, imbecile, eccentric and tottering;
You are thrice deformed.
Grandmother, your ugly face is wrapped in wrinkles.
Question your own thoughts and your mind examine.
You should practise the Buddha's Teaching,
You need a qualified and dependable Guru,
And then things may be different for you.

Your food and drink are cold and foul;
Your coat is heavy and in rags;
Your bed so rough it tears the skin;
These three are your constant companions.
Grandmother, you are now a wretch,
Half woman and half bitch!
Question your own thoughts and your mind examine!
You should practise the Buddha's Teaching,
What you need is a qualified and dependable Guru,
And then things may be different for you.

To attain higher birth and Liberation

Is harder than to see a star in daytime;
To fall into Samsaara's wretched path
Is easy and often happens.
Now, with fear and grief at heart,
You watch the time of death draw nigh.
Grandmother, can you face death with confidence?
Question your own mind and your thoughts examine!
What you need is to practise the Teaching of the Buddha,
What you need is a qualified and dependable Guru.

*

Milarepa said to his faithful patroness, Shindormo, "My dear patroness, except for advanced Dharma practitioners, the pains of birth, decay, illness and death descend upon everyone. It is good to think about and fear them, because this enables one to practise the Dharma when death is approaching." Whereupon he sang:

In the river of birth, decay, illness,
And death we worldly beings are submerged;
Who can escape these pains on earth?
We drift on with the tide.
Amidst waves of misery and darkness,
We flow on and on.
Seldom in Samsaara can one find joy.
More miseries come by trying to avoid them;
Through pursuing pleasures one's sins increase.
To be free from pain,
Wrong deeds should be shunned.
When death draws near, the wise
Always practise Dharma.

★

"I do not know how to observe the suffering of birth," said
Shindormo, "Please instruct me how to meditate upon it."
In answer, Milarepa sang:

My faithful patroness, I will,
Explain the suffering of birth.
The wanderer in the Bardo plane,
Is the Aalaya Consciousness,
Driven by lust and hatred,
It enters a mother's womb.

Therein it feels like a fish,
In a rock's crevice caught,
Sleeping in blood and yellow fluid,
It is pillowed in discharges,
Crammed in filth, it suffers pain.
A bad body from a bad Karma is born.

Though remembering past lives,
It cannot say a single word.
Now scorched by heat,
Now frozen by the cold,
In nine months it emerges,
From the womb in pain excruciating,
As if pulled out gripped by pliers.

When from the womb its head is squeezed,
The pain is like being thrown into a bramble pit.
The tiny body on the mother's lap,
Feels like a sparrow grappled by a hawk.
When from the baby's tender body,
The blood and filth are being cleansed,
The pain is like being flayed alive.
When the umbilical cord is cut,
It feels as though the spine was severed.
When wrapped in the cradle it feels bound,
By chains, imprisoned in a dungeon.

He who realises not the truth of No-arising,
Never can escape from the dread pangs of birth.

There is no time to postpone devotion:
When one dies one's greatest need,
Is the divine Dharma.
You should then exert yourself,
To practise Buddha's Teaching.

★

*Shindormo asked again, "Please preach for us the sufferings
of old age." In response, Milarepa sang:*

Listen, my good patrons, listen,
To the sufferings of old age.

Painful is it to see one's body,
Becoming frail and quite worn out.
Who can help but feel dismayed,
At the threat of growing old?
When old age descends upon one,
One's straight body becomes bent;
When one tries to step firmly,
One staggers against one's will;
One's black hairs turn white.
One's clear eyes grow dim;
One's head shakes with dizziness,
And one's keen ears turn deaf,
One's ruddy cheeks grow pale,
And one's blood dries up.

One's nose – the pillar of one's face – sinks in;
One's teeth – the essence of one's bones – protrude.
Losing control of tongue, one stammers.
On the approach of death,
One's anguish and debts grow.

One gathers food and friends,
But one cannot keep them,
Trying not to suffer,
One only suffers more,
When one tells the truth to people,
Seldom is one believed;
The sons and nephews one has raised,
And cherished, often become one's foes.
One gives away one's savings,
But wins no gratitude.
Unless you realise the truth of Non-decay,
You will suffer misery in old age.
He who when old neglects the Dharma,
Should know that he is bound by Karma.
It is good to practise,
The divine Dharma while you can still breathe.

★

Shindormo then said, "What you have just told us is very true; I have experienced these things myself. Now please preach for us the sufferings of sickness." In reply, Milarepa sang:

Dear patrons, you who know grief and sorrow,
Listen to the miseries of sickness.

This frail body is subject e'er to sickness,
So that one suffers excruciating pain.
The illnesses of Praana (mind), gall and phlegm,
Constantly invade this frail human body,
Causing its blood and matter to be heated;
The organs are thus gripped by pain.
In a safe and easy bed,
The sick man feels no comfort,
But turns and tosses, groaning in lament.
Through the Karma of (past) meanness,
Though with best of food you feed him,
He vomits all that he can take.
When you lay him in the cool,
He still feels hot and burning;
When you wrap him in warm cloth,
He feels cold as though soaked in sleet.
Though friends and kinsmen gather round,

None can relieve or share his pains,
Though warlocks and physicians are proficient,
They cannot help cases caused by Ripening Karma.

He who has not realised the truth of No-illness,
Much suffering must undergo.
Since we know not when sickness will strike,
It is wise to practise Holy Dharma –
The sure conqueror of illness!

*

"I hope to practise more Dharma when death draws near,"
said Shindormo, "now please preach for me the suffering of
death. " In answer, Milarepa sang:

Listen, my disheartened patroness:
Like the pain of repaying compound debts,
One must undergo the suffering of death,
Yama's guards catch and carry one,
When the time of death arrives.
The rich man cannot buy it off with money,
With his sword the hero cannot conquer it,
Nor can the clever woman outwit it by a trick.
Even the learned scholar cannot,
Postpone it with his eloquence.
Here, the unlucky cannot make appeal,
Nor can a brave man here display his valour.

When all the Nadis converge in the body,
One is crushed as if between two mountains –

All vision and sensation become dim.
When Bon priests and diviners become useless,
The trusted physician yields to his despair.
None can communicate with the dying man,
Protecting guards and devas vanish into nought.

Though the breath has not completely stopped,
One can all but smell the stale odour of dead flesh.
Like a lump of coal in chilly ashes,
One approaches to the brink of death.

When dying, some still count the dates and stars;
Others cry and shout and groan;
Some think of worldly goods;
Some, that their hard-earned wealth,
Will be enjoyed by others.

However deep one's love, or great one's sympathy,
He can but depart and journey on alone.
His good friend and consort,
Can only leave him there;
In a bundle his beloved body,
Will be folded and carried off,
Then thrown in water, burned in fire,
Or simply cast off in a desolate land.
Faithful patrons, what in the end can we retain?
Must we sit idly by and let all things go?
When your breath stops tomorrow,
No wealth on earth can help you.
Why, then, should one be mean?
Kind kinsmen circle round,
The bed of the dying,

But none can help him for a moment.
Knowing that all must be left behind,
One realises that all great love,
And attachment must be futile,
When that final moment comes,
Only Holy Dharma helps.

You should strive, dear patroness,
For a readiness to die!
Be certain and ready and when the time comes,
You will have no fear and no regret.

★

A married couple, in the village Mang Yul, had no children
and invited Milarepa to their house when he came that
way for alms. They sought to adopt him into their family
and said: "We have a good strip of land which we can give
you; you can then marry an attractive woman, and soon
you will have relatives." Milarepa replied, "I have no need
of these things and I will tell you why..."

Home and land at first seem pleasant;
But they are like a rasp filing away,
One's body, word and mind!
How toilsome ploughing and digging can become!
And when the seeds you planted never sprout,
You have worked for nought!
In the end it becomes a land of misery –
Desolate and unprotected –
A place for hungry spirits, and of haunting ghosts!
When I think of the warehouse,
For storing sinful deeds,
It gnaws at my heart,
In such a prison of transiency I will not stay,
I have no wish to join your family!

At first, when a man greets his relatives,
He is happy and joyful; with enthusiasm,

He serves, entertains and talks to them.
Later, they share his meat and wine.
He offers something to them once, they may reciprocate.

In the end, they cause anger, craving and bitterness;
They are a fountain of regret and unhappiness.
With this in mind, I renounce pleasant and sociable friends;
For kinsmen and neighbours, I have no appetite.

Wealth, at first, leads to self-enjoyment,
Making other people envious.
However much one has, one never feels it is enough,
Until one is bound by the miser's demon;
Hard it is then to spend it on virtuous deeds.

Wealth provokes enemies and stirs up ghosts.
One works hard to gather riches which others will spend;
In the end, one struggles for life and death,
To amass wealth and money invites enemies;
So I renounce the delusions of Samsaara.
To become the victim of deceitful devils,
I have no appetite.

★

*Milarepa was about to leave Nya Non for other
hermitages, but the patrons of that place besought him to
stay with the utmost earnestness. Milarepa replied: "If I do
not die, I shall try to come back to your village. If for some
time we cannot see each other, try at times to remember
and practise these things." Whereupon he sang:*

Alas, how pitiful are worldly things!
Like precious jade they cherish,
Their bodies, yet like ancient trees,
They are doomed in the end to fall.
Sometimes bridle your wild thoughts,
And pay heed to the Dharma.

Though you gather wealth,
As hard as bees collect their honey,
The ills that upon you may fall,
Can never be foretold,
Sometimes bridle your wild thoughts,
And pay heed to the Dharma.

One may offer to a Lama,
Loads of silk for many years;
But when an ill-fortune descends,
Like a fading rainbow,

One's faith at once dissolves.
Sometimes bridle your wild thoughts,
And pay heed to the Dharma.

Like a pair of mated beasts,
Lovers live together,
But calamity by the wolf's attack,
May fall on you at any time.
Sometimes bridle your wild thoughts,
And pay heed to the Dharma.

You may cherish your dear son,
Like a hen hatching her egg;
But a falling rock may crush it at any time.
Sometimes bridle your wild thoughts,
And pay heed to the Dharma.

A face may be as pretty as a flower,
Yet at any time it can be spoiled by violent hail.
Think at times of how this world,
Is sorry, transient and futile.

Though son and mother have affection,
For each other, when discords arise,
Like foes they clash and quarrel,
Sometimes towards all sentient beings,

You should feel compassion.

Basking in the warm sunlight,
May be pleasant and a comfort,
But a storm of woe may rise,
And choke you at any time,
Remember sometimes the deprived,
And give alms to those in need.

Oh, dear men and women patrons,
For him who cannot practise Dharma,
All his life will be meaningless,
All his acts wrong-doings!

*

*When Milarepa was staying in the Stone House of Drin,
Tsese, Ku Ju, and many other patrons came to him for
the Dharma. Tsese said, "Please give us some Buddhist
Teaching that is easy for us to understand." Milarepa
replied, "Very well, lend your ears and listen carefully
to this song."*

Dear patrons, with care listen,
For a moment to my words.
Superior men have need of Dharma;
Without it, they are like eagles –
Even though perched on high,
They have but little meaning.

Average men have need of Dharma;
Without it, they are like tigers –
Though possessing greatest strength,
They are of little value.
Inferior men have need of Dharma;
Without it, they are like a peddler's asses –
Though they carry a big load,
It does them but little good.

Superior women need the Dharma;
Without it, they are like pictures on a wall –
Though they look very pretty,
They have no use or meaning.

Average women need the Dharma;
Without it they are like little rats –
Though they are clever at getting food,
Their lives have but little meaning.

Inferior women need the Dharma;
Without it, they are just like vixens –
Though they be deft and cunning,
Their deeds have little value.

Old men need the Dharma;
Without it, they are like decaying trees.
Growing youths the Dharma need;
Without it, they are like yoked bulls.
Young maidens need the Dharma,
Without it, they are but decorated cows.
All young people need the Dharma;
Without it, they are as blossoms,
Shut within a shell.
All children need the Dharma;
Without it, they are as robbers possessed by demons.
Without the Dharma, all one does,
Lacks meaning and purpose.
Those who want to live with meaning
Should practise the Buddha's Teaching.

★

The King of Ye Rang and Ko Kom (in Nepal) had heard of Milarepa and sent his envoy to invite him to Nepal. As he declined to go the envoy expostulated that his Lord had got nothing except the envoy's empty hands and thorn-pricked feet. To this, Milarepa replied, "I am the great Universal Emperor. There is no other emperor who is happier, richer or more powerful than I."
The envoy retorted, "If you claim that you are the great Universal Emperor himself, then you must have Seven Precious Articles of Royalty. Please show me one of them."
Milarepa replied, "If you worldly kings and officers will follow my Royal Way, each of you may also become the Supreme Emperor, and thus be rich and noble."
Whereupon he sang:

If you kings and courtiers who seek pleasures,
Follow the Royal Succession of Milarepa,
Eventually you will obtain them.

This is the Royal Succession of Milarepa:
My faith is the Royal Precious Wheel,
Revolving 'round the virtues day and night.
My wisdom is the Royal Precious Gem,
Fulfilling all the wishes of myself and others.
The discipline's observance,

Is my Royal Precious Queen;
She is my adornment, one most beautiful.
Meditation is my Royal Precious Minister;
With him I accumulate the Two Provisions.
Self-inspection is my Royal Precious Elephant,
Which takes responsibility for Buddhist Dharma.

Diligence is my Royal Precious Horse,
Which bears the Klesas to Non-ego Land.
Study and contemplation is my Royal Precious General,
Who destroys the enemy of vicious thoughts.
If you have these Royal Precious Trappings,
You will gain a king's fame and prosperity,
And conquer all your foes.
You may then spread the Ten Virtues in your dominion,
And urge all mother-like sentient beings,
To follow my noble teachings.

*

*At Gung Tang Castle, some men were building a house and
Milarepa approached them for alms. Saying that they had
no time and were busy while he appeared to be idle, they
invited him to join in their house construction.
But Milarepa declined to work upon worldly building, for
he said his house was already constructed in his own way.
The men asked him, "How did you build your house, and
why do you spurn our work so strongly?"
Milarepa sang in reply:*

Faith is the firm foundation of my house,
Diligence forms the high walls,
Meditation makes the huge bricks,
And Wisdom is the great corner-stone.
With these four things I build my castle,
And it will last as long as the Truth eternal!
Your worldly houses are delusions,
Mere prisons for the demons,
And so I would abandon and desert them.

★

Some demons had come to afflict Milarepa, but after he
had sung two songs to them they began to turn towards
the Dharma. They said: "We are most grateful for your
preaching on the truth of Karma. In all frankness, we are of
limited intelligence and limitless ignorance. Our minds are
steeped in a morass of stubborn habitual thoughts. Pray,
therefore, teach us a lesson profound in meaning, great
in profit, and simple in comprehension and observation."
Milarepa then sang…

The Song of the Seven Truths

However beautiful a song's words may be,
It is but a tune to those,
Who grasp not the words of Truth.
If a parable agrees not with the Buddha's Teaching,
However eloquent it may sound,
'Tis but a booming echo.
If one does not practise Dharma,
However learned in the Doctrines one may claim to be,
One is only self-deceived.
Living in solitude is self-imprisonment,
If one practises not the instruction,
Of the Oral Transmission.
Labour on the farm is but self-punishment,

If one neglects the teaching of the Buddha.

For those who do not guard their morals,
Prayers are but wishful thinking.
For those who do not practise what they preach,
Oratory is but faithless lying.
Wrong-doing shunned, sins of themselves diminish;
Good deeds done and merit will be gained.
Remain in solitude, and meditate alone,
Much talking is of no avail,
Follow what I sing, and practise Dharma!

★

*The people of Nya Non, hearing that Milarepa had decided
to go, brought him good offerings and besought him to
stay. However, Milarepa replied, "I am going to another
place to await the coming of my death. If I do not die
soon, there will always be a chance for us to meet again. In
the meantime, you should all try to practise these things,"
and he sang to them of the Six Paaramitaa
and their applications:*

Obeisance to my perfect Guru!
Property and possessions,
Are like dew on the grass –
Give them away without avarice.
A human body that can practise Dharma
Is most precious –
(To attain it again), you should keep the precepts well
As if protecting your own eyes!

Anger brings one to the Lower Realms,
So, never lose your temper,
Even though your life be forfeit.
Inertia and slackness,
Never bring accomplishment –
Exert yourself therefore in devotion.

Through distractions Mahaayaana,
Can never be understood,
Practise therefore concentration.

Since Buddhahood cannot be won without,
Watch the nature of your mind within.

Like fog is faith unstable,
When it starts to fade, you should,
Strengthen it more than ever.

★

Milarepa cautioned his disciple Rechungpa to live as he had lived, saying, "You should renounce all Eight Worldly Desires and meditate hard while you still have the chance. Now listen to my song."

Remember how your Guru lived,
And bear in mind his honeyed words.
He who wastes a chance for Dharma,
Will never have another.

Bear, then, in mind the Buddha's Teaching,
And practise it with perseverance,
By clinging to things of this life,
In the next, one suffers more.
If you crave for pleasures,
Your troubles but increase.

One is indeed most foolish,
To miss a chance for Dharma.
Practise hard in fear of death!
Committing sins will draw,
You to the Lower Realms.
By pretending and deceiving,
You cheat and mislead yourself.
Merits diminish,
With the growth of evil thoughts.

If you are concerned with future life,
Diligently practise your devotions,
A yogi longing for good clothes,
Will soon lose his mind;
A yogi yearning for good food,
Will soon do bad deeds;
A yogi loving pleasant words,
Will not gain, but lose.
Renounce worldly pursuits, Rechungpa,
Devote yourself to meditation.

If you try to get a patron,
Who is rich, you will meet a foe.
He who likes to be surrounded,
By crowds, will soon be disappointed,
He who hoards much wealth and money,
Soon is filled with vicious thoughts.

Meditate, my son Rechungpa,
And put your mind into the Dharma.

Realisation will be won,
At last by him who practises;
He who cannot practise,
But only talks and brags,
Is always telling lies.

Alas, how hard it is to find,
The chance and time to practise long,
Rechungpa, try to meditate without diversions.

If you merge your mind with Dharma,
You will e'er be gay and joyful;
You will always find it better,
If oft you dwell in solitude.
Son Rechungpa, may the precious,
Illuminating-Void samaadhi,
Remain forever in your mind!

★

Rechungpa had a wish to visit Central Tibet (Weu) but
Milarepa tried to dissuade him from going by saying that
it was not yet the right time for him to leave his Guru.
But Rechungpa still kept pressing his request. Whereupon
Milarepa sang:

It is good for you, the white lion on the mountain,
To stay high, and never go deep into the valley,
Lest your beautiful mane be sullied!
To keep it in good order,
You should remain on the high snow mountain.
Rechungpa, hearken to my words today!

It is good for you, the great eagle, on high rocks,
To perch, and never fall into a pit,
Lest your mighty wings be damaged!
To keep them in good order,
You should remain in the high hills.
Rechungpa, hearken to your Guru's words!

It is good for you, the jungle tiger,
To stay in the deep forest: if you rove,
About the plain, you will lose your dignity!
To keep your splendour in perfection,
In the forest you should remain.

Rechungpa, hearken to your Guru's words!

It is good for you, the golden-eyed fish,
To swim in the central sea;
If you swim too close to the shore,
You will in a net be caught.
You should remain in the deep waters.
Rechungpa, hearken to your Guru's words!
It is good for you, Rechungpa of Gung Tang,
For you to stay in hermitages;
If you wander in different places,
Your experience and realisation will dim.
To protect and cultivate devotion
You should remain in the mountains.
Rechungpa, hearken to your Guru's words!

★

Drashi Tse, a patron, once asked Milarepa: "Do you think I should concentrate my effort on meditation alone, or not?" Milarepa replied, "It is for the very sake of practice that the Dharma is preached and studied. If one does not practise or meditate, both studying and preaching will be meaningless."

Hearken, my faithful patrons!
Even sinful persons,
Not knowing the great power of Karma,
Dream of achieving Liberation,
Life wears out as days and years go by,
Yet in pursuing pleasures,
People spend their lives.
They ask, will this month or year be good?"
Blind to life's speedy passing,
Fools cherish foolish questions.
He who truly wants to practise Dharma,
Should make offerings to the Holy Ones,
Take Refuge in the Triple Gem,
Give service to the Jetsun Guru,
Pay respect to his parents,
Give alms without hoping for reward.
He should offer help to those in need,
He should live and act up to The Dharma's principles.
Not much is needed for Buddhist practice;

Too many vows lead to self-cheating.
Dear patrons, try to practise what I say.

Milarepa said: "Many people think that they will have
ample time to practise the Dharma, but without their
notice or expectation, death suddenly descends upon
them and they lose forever the chance to practise. What
then can they do? One should turn all one's Buddhist
knowledge inside one's mouth, and then meditate. If one
does not further one's studies and meditation at the same
time, but thinks that one should first learn a great deal
before starting the actual practice (one will be completely
lost) because knowledge is infinite, and there is no
possibility of mastering it all."

★

Some patrons had made copious offerings to Rechungpa
before his departure for Weu but had offered his old
teacher, Milarepa, only third-rate provisions. Milarepa
came to know of this and shamed them to their faces,
whereupon they felt guilt and deep regret. One day they
came again and brought excessive offerings saying, "Please
sing for us to awaken our insight into the transiency of
beings." Milarepa would not accept their offerings but
he sang this for them:

Hearken you mean patrons!
For the sake of fame, to do,
Meritorious deeds –
For this life's sake to seek,
The protection of Buddha –
To give alms for the sake,
Of returns and dividends –
To serve and offer for the sake,
Of vanity and pride –
These four ways will never requite one!

For the sake of gluttony,
To hold a sacramental feast –
For the sake of egotism,
To strive for Sutra-learning –

For distraction and amusement,
To indulge in foolish talk and song –
For vain glory's sake,
To give the Initiations –
These four ways will never bring one blessings!

If for love of preaching one expounds,
Without the backing of scripture,
If through self-conceit,
One accepts obeisance;
If like a bungling, fumbling fool one teaches,
Not knowing the disciple's capacity,
If to gather money one behaves,
Like a Dharma practiser –
These four ways can never help the welfare of sentient beings!
To prefer diversions to solitude,
To love pleasures and hate hardship,
To crave for talk when urged to meditate,
To wallow arrogantly in the world –
These four ways will never bring one to Liberation!

This is the song of Fourfold Warning,
Dear patrons, bear it in your minds!

*

*Rechungpa had just returned from India complete
with new learning, instructions in various meditations,
skill in logic, and a swollen head. In order to clear up
Rechungpa's pride and arrogance, Milarepa sang:*

...Oh, my son, your pride in what you learned,
Will lead you well astray!

To preach a lot, with empty words,
Ruins your good experience and meditation.

To be swollen with pride and arrogance,
Proves you have betrayed the Guru's precepts.
Nothing gives cause for more regret,
Than disobedience to the Guru,
No one is more distracted and confused,
Than he who ceases to meditate in solitude.
Nothing is more fruitless,
Than a Buddhist who renounces not his kin.
Nothing is more shameful,
Than a learned Buddhist who neglects his meditation.
Nothing is more disgraceful,
Than a monk who violates the rules.

★

More advice sung by Milarepa to try to cure
Rechungpa's pride:

It is fine that father and son are in harmony –
Maintaining harmony with people is a great merit;
But the best merit is to keep in harmony,
With one's father.
If one is discordant with all the people he knows,
He must be a person ominous or obnoxious.
Yet even more ominous is discord between father and son.

Good it is to maintain harmony with one's
Father by right deeds,
Good it is to repay one's mother's kindness and bounties,
Good it is to act in concord with all.

One's wish can be fulfilled,
If one is on good terms with one's brothers,
To please one's Guru,
Is to gain his blessings;
To be humble is to succeed,
A good Buddhist is one who conquers all bad dispositions.
Kindness, is toleration of slanders;
To be modest is to gain fame and popularity;
To maintain pure discipline,

Is to do away with pretence and concealment;
To live with a sage is to gain improvement;
To be indifferent is to stop all gossip;
To be good and compassionate is to advance,
One's Bodhi-mind.
These are things that a wise man should do,
But a fool can never distinguish friend from foe.

★

Another exhortation to Rechungpa:

Listen, Rechung Dorjedrapa,
The well-learned Buddhist scholar.
Listen, and think with care on what I say,
Before faith and yearning arise for Dharma,
Beg not alms for mere enjoyment.
Before you have realised primordial Truth,
Boast not of your sublime philosophy.
Before you have fully mastered the Awareness within,
Engage not in blind and foolish acts.
Before you can feed on the Instructions,
Involve yourself not in wicked occultism.
Before you can explain the profound Teaching,
Be not beguiled by partial knowledge.
Before you can increase your merits,
Dispute not over others' goods.
Before you can destroy your inner cravings,
Treat not charity as if it were your right.
Before you can stop projecting habitual thoughts,
Guess not when you make predictions.
Before you have gained Supreme Enlightenment,
Assume not that you are a venerable Lama,
Before you can master all virtues and practices,
Consider not leaving your Guru.
Son Rechungpa, it is better not to go, but stay!

★

A yogi of Gu Tang, who had great faith in Milarepa,
requested for meditation instructions. After these had been
given, he said: "To help ignorant men like us, pray now,
instruct us in the practice of the Six Paaramitaas."
Milarepa sang in reply:

Property and wealth are like dew on grass;
Knowing this, gladly should one give them away. (*charity*)

It is most precious to be born a leisured and,
Worthy human being,
Knowing this, one should with care observe the precepts,
As if protecting one's own eyes. (*moral discipline*)

Anger is the cause of falling to the Realms Below;
Knowing this, one should refrain from wrath,
Even at the risk of life. (*patience*)

Benefit to oneself and to others,
Can never be achieved through sloth;
Strive, therefore, to do good deeds. (*diligence*)

A perturbed, wandering mind,
Never sees the truth of Mahaayaana;
Practise, therefore, concentration. (*meditation*)

The Buddha cannot be found through searching;
So contemplate your own mind. (*wisdom*)

Until the autumn mists dissolve into the sky,
Strive on with faith and determination.

*Two scholar-bhikkhus came to argue about the
Dharma with Milarepa but the discussion (which was a
demonstration of his mastery of meditation) turned against
them. Upon which, one of them asked for his instruction
in the Six Paaramitaas. In answer, Milarepa sang:*

If from parsimony one cannot free oneself,
What is the use of discussing charity? (*daana*)
If one does not forswear hypocrisy and pretence,
What is the use of keeping discipline? (*sila*)
If one abjures not malicious revilings,
What is the use of exercising,
pretentious "patience"? (*khanti*)
If one abandons not indifference and inertness,
What is the use of swearing to be Moral? (*viriya*)
If one conquers not the errant thoughts within,
What is the use of toiling in meditation? (*samaadhi*)
If one does not see all forms as helpful,
What is the use of practising the Wisdom (*paññaa*)
If one knows not the profound teaching,
Of forbidding and allowing,
What is the use of learning?

If one knows not the art of taking and rejecting,
What is the use of speaking on Karma-causation?

If one's mind does not accord with the Dharma,
What is the use of joining the Order?
If the poisonous snake of Klesa is not killed,
The yearning for wisdom only leads to fallacy.
If venomous jealousy is not overcome,
One's yearning for the Bodhi-mind will be an illusion.
If one refrains not from hurting people,
One's longing for respect and honour,
Is merely wishful thinking.
If one cannot conquer ego-clinging and prejudice,
One's craving for the Equality of Dharma,
Only brings wrong views.
If one cannot subdue the demon, clinging-ego,
One's Klesas will be great and his Yoga bound to fail.
If one's actions conform not with the Dharma.
One will always hinder the good deeds of others.
If one has not yet absorbed one's mind in Dharma,
One's babbling and prattling will only disturb others' minds.
Therefore, do not waste your life in words and chatter,
But try to gain the assurance of no-regret,
And the confidence of facing death!

★

Milarepa said: "Dear teachers, the proverb says: 'Judging from the complexion of his face, one knows whether a man has eaten or not'. In the same light, the fact that one knows or knows not the Dharma, can easily be detected by whether or not one can conquer one's own ego-clinging desires. If he can, that proves that one knows and practises the Buddhist Teachings. One may be very eloquent talking about the Dharma and win all the debates, but if one cannot subdue even a fraction of one's ego-clinging and desires, but merely indulges oneself in words and talk, one's victories in debates will never bring one any profit but will only increase one's egotism and pride."

★

One of the scholar-bhikkhus who had previously been
opposed to Milarepa, gradually acquired faith in him and
eventually came to him for the Dharma, requesting, "Now
please be kind enough to instruct me in the essence of the
Six Paaramitaas." In response, Milarepa sang:

I am not well-versed in words,
Being no scholar-preacher,
Yet this petitioner is sincere and good.
The Six Paaramitaas contain all Buddhist teachings.
To those who practise Dharma,
Wealth is but a cause of diversion.
He who gives his (wealth) all away,
Will be born a Prince of Heaven.
Noble is it to practise charity!
Moral discipline is a ladder to Liberation,
Which neither monks nor laymen can discard,
All Buddhist followers should practise it!
Buddhist patience, by the Patience-preacher,
Exemplified,
Is the virtue which the Buddha cherished most,
It is a garment difficult to wear,
Yet all merits grow when it is worn.

Diligence is the short path to Freedom,
And a necessity for Dharma-practice.

Without it nothing can be done.
Ride then upon the horse of diligence!

These four Dharmas bring merit to men,
Being indispensable for all.
Now I will speak of Wisdom.
Meditation is a teaching between these two,
As it applies both to Wisdom and Merit practice,
By it all distractions are overcome,
For all Buddhist practice, it is most important.
Wisdom-Paaramitaa is the teaching of Final Truth,
The dearest treasure of all Buddhas.
Enjoy it then without exhaustion,
It is the Wish-fulfilling Gem of Heaven,
Fulfilling the hopes of all sentient beings.
To those who can renounce activities,
Wisdom-Paaramitaa will bring final rest.
This provision of Wisdom is most precious;
Whereby one will reach perfection step by step.

This is my reply, Venerable Monk,
Remember and practise it with joy!

*

Upon Mount Bonbo, Milarepa instructed many Repas who were preparing to depart for meditation in distant hermitages. Those junior Repas who wanted to stay with him, then said to him, "We are now in an age of defilement. For the sake of inferior and slow-witted persons like us, please preach something appropriate to our needs." In response, Milarepa sang:

Hearken further, my Son-disciples!

At this time of defilement,
That shadows the Dharma of Sakyamuni,
One should strive with perseverance,
And carve upon one's mind-stone,
The word, "Diligence".
When you feel sleepy during Meditation, try,
To pray hard with your awakened body, mouth and mind.
When the fire-spark of Wisdom dims, try,
To inflame it with the wind of Mindfulness.
If you want to be freed from Samsaara's prison,
Practise hard without diversion.
If to Nirvana you aspire,
Abandon then this world.
If from the depths of your heart,
You want to practise Dharma,

Listen to my words and follow in my footsteps.
If you want to consummate the (Supreme)
Accomplishment,
Never forget that death will come.
If hard and long you meditate, all Buddhas,
In the past, the present and the future,
Will be well-pleased.
If you are ever straight-forward and upright in the Dharma,
You will receive the grace of your Guru.
If without error you understand these words,
You can be sure that more happiness,
And joy will come your way,
For such is my experience.

*

Some devas invited Milarepa to preach the Dharma in
Heaven but he cautioned them saying, "You must know
that Heaven is far from dependable; it is not eternal, and
one should not rely on it. To be born in Heaven is not
necessarily a wonderful thing." The Devas of Heaven said,
"In ignorant beings like us, the Klesas always follow the
mind. Pray give us a teaching with which we can correct
this fault, so that we may depend upon it and practise it
frequently." In response to their request, Milarepa sang:

Should you, oh faithful lady Devas,
Intend to practise the Dharma often,
Inwardly you should practise concentration,
And contemplation.
The renunciation of external affairs is your adornment.
Oh, bear in mind this remedy for external involvement!
With self-composure and mindfulness,
You should remain serene.
Glory is the equanimity of your mind and speech!
Glory is the resignation from many actions!

Should you meet disagreeable conditions,
Disturbing to your mind,
Keep watch upon yourself and be alert;
Keep warning yourself:
"The danger of anger is on its way".
When you meet with enticing wealth,

Keep watch upon yourself and be alert,
Keep a check upon yourself,
"The danger of craving is on its way".

Should hurtful, insulting words come to your ears,
Keep watch upon yourself and be alert,
And so remind yourself:
"Hurtful sounds are but delusions of the ear".
When you associate with your friends,
Watch carefully and warn yourself,
"Let not jealousy in my heart arise!"

When you are plied with services and offerings.
Be alert and warn yourself:
"Let me beware lest pride should spring up in my heart!"

At all times, in every way, keep watch upon yourself.
At all times try to conquer evil thoughts within you!
Whatever you may meet in your daily doings,
You should contemplate its void and illusory nature.

Were even one hundred saints and scholars gathered here,
More than this they could not say.
May you all be happy and prosperous!
May you all, with joyful hearts,
Devote yourselves to the practice of the Dharma!

✦

A young shepherd by the name of Sanje Jhap, who was sixteen years old, became interested in knowing what his mind really was. Milarepa tested his ability by instructing him to go for Refuge to the Three Precious Ones and then to visualize a Buddha-image in front of his nose. The boy was not seen for seven days and his father feared that he was dead. They found him in a clay pit sitting upright and asked him why he had not returned home for seven days. The boy said that they must be joking for he had only been there a short time – but it was seven days. While giving him instructions Milarepa sang to him about his mind:

Listen to me, dear shepherd, the protector (of sheep)!
By merely hearing of the taste of sugar,
Sweetness cannot be experienced,
Though one's mind may understand,
What sweetness is,
It cannot experience it directly,
Only the tongue can know it.
In the same way, one cannot see in full the nature of mind,
Though he may have a glimpse of it,
If it has been pointed out by others,
If one relies not on this one glimpse,
But continues searching for the nature of mind,
He will see it fully in the end.
Dear shepherd, in this way you should observe your mind.

Listen to me, young shepherd.
The body is between the conscious and unconscious state,
While the mind is the crucial and decisive factor!
He who feels sufferings in the Lower Realms,
Is the prisoner of Samsaara,
Yet it is the mind that can free you from Samsaara.
Surely you want to reach the other shore?
Surely you long for the City of Well-being and Liberation?
If you desire to go, dear child,
I can show the Way to you,
And give you the instructions.

✱

Upon Rechungpa's return from India, with books on logic,
incantations from outsiders and much pride, as well as
genuine meditation instructions, Milarepa decided to
rescue him from this evil and so to welcome him, he sang:

I am a yogi who lives on the snow mountain peak,
With a healthy body I glorify the Mandala of the Whole.
Cleansed of vanity from the Five Poisons,
I am not unhappy;
I feel nought but joy!
Renouncing all turmoil,
And fondness for diversion,
I reside alone in perfect ease.
Forswearing the bustle of this world,
Joyfully I stay in no-man's land.
Since I have left embittered family life,
I no longer have to earn and save;
Since I want no books,
I do not intend to be a learned man;
Since I practise virtuous deeds,
I feel no shame of heart.
Since I have no pride or vanity,
I renounce with joy the saliva-splashing debate!
Hypocrisy I have not, nor pretension.
Happy and natural I live,
Without forethought or adjustment.

Since I want no fame nor glory,
Rumours and accusations disappear.
Where'er I go, I feel happy,
Whate'er I wear, I feel joyful,
Whatever food I eat, I am satisfied.
I am always happy.
Through Marpa's grace,
I, your old father, Milarepa,
Have realised Samsaara and Nirvana.
The Yoga of joy ever fills my hermitage.
Your Repa brothers are well;
On hills remote they make progress in their meditations.
Oh, my son Rechungpa,
Have you returned from India?
Did you feel tired and weary on the journey?
Has your mind been sharpened and refreshed?
Has your voice been good for singing?
Did you practise and follow your Guru's instructions?
Did you secure the teachings that you wanted?
Did you obtain all the various instructions?
Have you gained much knowledge and much learning?
Have you noticed your pride and egotism?
Are you altruistic in your thoughts and actions?
This is my song of welcoming for you,
On your return.

★

*Five young nuns from Mon had become Milarepa's
disciples. Having dwelt with him for some time, they
decided to invite him to their village (whence they thought
of returning). They said to him: "Revered One, since
your mind no longer changes, there is no need for you
to practise meditation. Therefore, for the sake of sentient
beings please come to our village and preach the Dharma
for us." Milarepa replied, "Practising meditation in solitude
is, in itself, a service to the people. Although my mind no
longer changes, it is still a good tradition for a great yogi to
remain in solitude." He then sang:*

Through the practice (of meditation),
I show gratitude to my Guru.
Pray grant me your grace, ripen and liberate me.

You gifted disciples, followers of Dharma,
Heed carefully, with all attention,
While I sing of the profound Essential Teaching.

The Great Lioness of the upper snow mountain,
Poses proudly on the summit of the peak;
She is not afraid –
Proudly dwelling on the mountain,
Is the snow lion's way.

The Queen Vulture on Red Rock,
Stretches her wings in the wide sky,
She is not afraid of falling –
Flying through the sky is the vulture's way.

In the depths of the great ocean,
Darts the een of fish, glittering;
She is not afraid (of drowning) –
Swimming is the fish's way.

On the branches of the oak trees,
Agile monkeys swing and leap,
They are not afraid of falling –
Such is the wild monkey's way.

Under the leafy canopy of the dense wood,
The striped tiger roams and swiftly runs,
Not because of fear or worry –
This shows her haughty pride,
And is the mighty tiger's way.

In the wood on Singa Mountain,
I, Milarepa, meditate on voidness,
Not because I fear to lose my understanding –
Constant meditation is the yogi's way.

Those great yogis who have mastered the Practice,
Never desire anything in this world.
It is not because they want fame,
That they remain in solitude;
It is the natural sign springing from their hearts –
The true feeling of non-attachment and renunciation.

Yogis who practise the teaching of the Path Profound,
Dwell always in caves and on mountains,
Not that they are cynical or pompous,
But to concentrate on meditation is their self-willing.
I, the cotton-clad, have sung many songs,
Not to amuse myself by singing sophistries,
But for your sake, faithful followers who assemble here,
From my heart I have spoken words helpful and profound.

★

A monk-disciple of Milarepa, Ligor Sharu, wanted Milarepa
to adapt himself somewhat to worldly conventions, so
as to win the interest and following of great scholars.
Milarepa refused this idea saying that he would ever follow
his Guru's instructions to live remotely, and
he sang to Ligor Sharu:

I bow down to Marpa, the Translator.

Realising that fame is as unreal as an echo,
I abandon not the ascetic way of life,
Throwing away all cares and preparations.
Whatever reputation I may have,
I shall always be happy and contented.

Realising that all things are illusion,
I cast away possessions;
For wealth obtained by strife I have not the least desire!
Whatever my means and prestige,
I shall always be happy and contented.

Realising that all followers are phantoms,
I have no concern for human relationship,
And travel where I please,
Unlike those artificial scholar-priests,

Who act with discretion and restraint.
Whatever the status I may have,
I shall always be happy and contented.

Realising that desires and sufferings,
Are themselves the Great Equality,
I cut the rope of passion and of hatred.
With or without associates,
I shall always be happy and contented.

The nature of being is beyond play-words;
Attachments to any doctrine or concept,
Is merely a matter of self-confusion.
Unshackling the fetter of the knower-and-the-known,
Whatever I become and wherever I remain,
I shall always be happy and contented.

In the great Illuminating Mind itself,
I see no pollution by wandering thoughts.
Throwing away all reasonings and observations,
Whatever words I hear and say,
I shall always be happy and contented.

★

Rechungpa first went to India to be cured of leprosy, and
before he went he sealed up with clay the mouth of the
cave where Milarepa was meditating. When he returned
having been cured, people said that the yogi Mila had not
been seen for some time. Rechungpa went to the cave and
broke down the wall, which was still intact. Milarepa was
still in meditation, and then sang to him as a greeting:

I bow down at the feet of Marpa, the Gracious One.

Because I have left my kinsmen, I am happy;
Because I have abandoned attachment to my country,
I am happy;
Since I disregard this place,
I am happy;
As I do not wear the lofty garb of priesthood,
I am happy;

Because I cling not to house and family, I am happy;
I need not this or that, so I am happy.
Because I possess the great wealth of Dharma, I am happy;
Because I worry not about property, I am happy;
Because I have no fear of losing anything, I am happy;
Since I never dread exhaustion, I am happy;

Having fully realised Mind-Essence, I am happy;
As I need not force myself to please my patrons,
I am happy;
Having no fatigue or weariness, I am happy;
As I need prepare for nothing, I am happy;
Since all I do complies with Dharma, I am happy,
Never desiring to move, I am happy;
As the thought of death brings me no fear, I am happy;
Bandits, thieves and robbers never molest me,
So at all times I am happy!
Having won the best conditions for Dharma-practice,
I am happy;
Having ceased from evil deeds and left off sinning,
I am happy;
Treading the Path of Merits, I am happy;
Divorced from hate and injury, I am happy,
Having lost all pride and jealousy, I am happy;
Understanding the wrongness of the Eight Worldly Winds,
I am happy;
Absorbed in quiet and even-mindedness, I am happy,
Using the mind to watch the mind, I am happy;
Without hope or fear, I am happy,
In the sphere of Non-clinging Illuminations,
I am happy;
The Non-distinguishing Wisdom of Dharmadhatu,
Is itself happy;

Poised in the natural realm of Immanence,
I am happy;
In letting the Six Groups of Consciousness go by,
To return to their original nature, I am happy;

The five radiant gates of sense all make one happy;
To stop the mind that comes and goes is happy,
Oh, I have so much of happiness and joy!
This is a song of gaiety I sing,
This is a song of gratitude to my Guru and the,
Three Precious Ones –
I want no other happiness.

Through the grace of Buddha and the Gurus,
Food and clothes are provided by my patrons.
With no bad deeds and sins,
I shall be joyful when I die;
With all good deeds and virtues,
I am happy while alive.
Enjoying yoga, I am indeed most happy.
But how are you, Rechungpa?
Is your wish fulfilled?

★

*The envoy of the Nepali King, upon meeting him for the
first time, was wonderstruck at Milarepa's lack of material
possessions and asked him: "Don't you find it hard to live
thus without taking nourishing food? Why is it necessary
to abandon all belongings?" Milarepa then answered
the envoy: "I am the Tibetan yogi, Milarepa. 'Without
belongings' means 'without sufferings'."
Now listen to my song:*

I bow down to all holy Gurus.

I am the man called Milarepa.
For possessions I have no desire.
Since I never strive to make money,
First I do not suffer,
Because of making it;
Then I do not suffer,
Because of keeping it;
In the end I do not suffer,
Because of hoarding it.
Better far and happier is it,
Not to have possessions.
Without attachment to kinsmen and companions,
I do not seek affection in companionship,
First I do not suffer,

Because of heart-clinging;
Then I do not suffer
From any quarrelling;
In the end I do not suffer,
Because of separation.
It is far better to have no affectionate companions.

Since I have no pride and egotism,
I do not look for fame and glory.
First I do not suffer,
Because of seeking them;
Then I do not suffer,
In trying to preserve them;
In the end I do not suffer,
For fear of losing them.
It is far better to have neither fame nor glory.
Since I have no desire for any place,
I crave not to be here, nor there.
First I do not worry,
About my home's protection,
Then I do not suffer,
From a fervent passion for it;
In the end I am not anxious to defend it.
It is far better to have neither home nor land.

★

*This is the song for some patrons from Drin who were
ashamed because of Milarepa's lack of
conventional behaviour:*

Through wandering long in many places,
I have forgotten my native land.

Staying long with my Holy Jetsun,
I have forgotten all my kinsmen.
Keeping for long the Buddha's Teaching,
I have forgotten worldly things.
Staying for long in hermitages,
I have forgotten all diversions.
Through long watching of monkeys' play,
I have forgotten sheep and cattle.
Long accustomed to a tinder-box,
I have forgotten all household chores.
Long used to solitude without servant or master,
I have forgotten courteous manners.
Long accustomed to be carefree,
I have forgotten worldly shame.
Long accustomed to the mind coming and going,
By itself, I have forgotten how to hide things.
Long used to burning Duma-heat,
I have forgotten clothing.

Long accustomed to practising Non-discriminating Wisdom,
I have forgotten all distracting thoughts.
Long used to practising the Two-in-One Illumination,
I have forgotten all nonsensical ideas.
These twelve 'oblivions' are the teachings of this yogi.
Why, dear patrons, do you not also follow them?
I have untied the knot of dualism;
What need have I to follow your customs.
To me, Bodhi is spontaneity itself!

The Dharma of you worldly people,
Is too difficult to practise.
Caring for nought, I live the way I please.
Your so-called 'shame' only brings deceit,
And fraud; How to pretend I know not.

*

*In a gathering of patrons, a young man said to Milarepa:
"We would like to come to you for instructions; please
tell us where your temple is and who provides your
sustenance." In answer Milarepa sang:*

My temple is an unnamed hermitage,
My patrons are men and women everywhere,
No one can tell where I go or stay.
In the caves where no man comes,
I, the yogi, am lost to view.
(When I travel) I carry,
Only my Guru's Instructions – lighter,
Than feathers, I shoulder them with ease;
More handy than gold, I conceal them where I please,
Stronger than a solid castle,
In all perils they stand firm.
In the three winters I dwell happily in forests;
In the three summers I stay cheerfully on snow mountains;
In the three springs I live with pleasure in the marshes;
In the three autumns I wander joyfully for alms.
In the teaching of my Guru, my mind is always happy;
Singing songs of inspiration, my mouth is always happy,
Wearing cotton from Nepal, my body's always happy.
In delight I accomplish all and everything –
To me there is but cheer and joy.

★

*The patrons of Nya Non wished Milarepa to stay with
them permanently. Milarepa replied, "I cannot stay here
long, but I will bestow the blessing of long life and good
health upon all of you. Also I will make a wish that we
meet again under auspicious circumstances conducive to
the Dharma." Then he sang:*

In the immense blue sky above,
Roll on the sun and moon.
Their courses mark the change of time.
Blue sky, I wish you health and fortune,
For I, the moon-and-sun, am leaving,
To visit the Four Continents for pleasure.

On the mountain peak is a great rock,
'Round which circles oft the vulture,
The King of birds.
Their meeting,
And their parting mark the change of time.
Dear rock, be well and healthy, for I,
The vulture, now will fly away,
Into the vast space for pleasure.
May lightnings never strike you,
May I not be caught by snares.
Inspired by the Dharma,

May we soon meet again,
In prosperity and boon.

Below in the Tsang River,
Swim fish with golden eyes;
Their meeting and their parting,
Mark the change of time.
Dear stream, be well and healthy, for I,
The fish, am going to the Ganges for diversion.
May irrigators never drain you,
May fishermen ne'er net me,
Inspired by the Dharma,
May we soon meet again,
In prosperity and boon.

In the fair garden blooms the flower, Halo;
Circling round it is the Persian bee.
Their meeting and their parting,
Mark the change of time.
Dear flower, be well and healthy, for I,
Will see the Ganges' blooms for pleasure.
May hail not beat down upon you,
May winds blow me not away.
Inspired by the Dharma,
May we soon meet again,
In prosperity and boon.

Circling round the Yogi Milarepa,
Are the faithful patrons from Nya Non;
Their meeting and their parting,
Mark the change of time.
Be well and healthy, dear patrons, as I,
Leave for the far mountains for diversion.
May I, the yogi, make good progress,
And you, my patrons, all live long.
Inspired by the Dharma,
May we soon meet again,
In prosperity and boon!